MACMILLAN
INTERMEDIATE

CHARLES DICKENS

The Old Curiosity Shop

Retold by Helen Holwill

MACMILLAN

MACMILLAN READERS
INTERMEDIATE LEVEL

Founding Editor: John Milne

The Macmillan Readers provide a choice of enjoyable reading materials for learners of English. The series is published at six levels – Starter, Beginner, Elementary, Pre-intermediate, Intermediate and Upper.

Level Control
Information, structure and vocabulary are controlled to suit the students' ability at each level.

The number of words at each level:

Starter	about 300 basic words
Beginner	about 600 basic words
Elementary	about 1100 basic words
Pre-intermediate	about 1400 basic words
Intermediate	about 1600 basic words
Upper	about 2200 basic words

Vocabulary
Some difficult words and phrases in this book are important for understanding the story. Some of these words are explained in the story, some are shown in the pictures and others are marked with a number like this: ...[3]. Phrases are marked with [P]. Words with a number are explained in the *Glossary* at the end of the book and phrases are explained on the *Useful Phrases* pages.

Answer Keys
Answer Keys for the *Points For Understanding* and *Exercises* sections can be found at www.macmillanenglish.com/readers.

Audio Download
There is an audio download available to buy for this title. Visit www.macmillanenglish.com/readers for more information.

Contents

	A Note About The Author	*4*
	A Note About The Story	*5*
	The People In The Story	*7*
1	The Old Curiosity Shop	8
2	Unwanted Visitors	11
3	Fred and Richard Make a Plan	17
4	Quilp Uncovers a Secret	19
5	Everything Changes	23
6	The Long Journey Begins	27
7	A New Beginning for Kit	31
8	Chance Meetings	35
9	Nell Gets a Job	38
10	Nell has a Terrible Shock	41
11	Richard Gets a Job	45
12	The Single Gentleman	48
13	Nell is Given Hope	51
14	Quilp Makes a Plan	54
15	A Village Life	57
16	There are Problems for Kit	59
17	There is Hope for Kit	66
18	Quilp's Luck Changes	68
19	The Single Gentleman Shares his Story	71
20	Nell and her Grandfather are Found	75
21	The End	79
	Points For Understanding	*81*
	Glossary	*89*
	Useful Phrases	*97*
	Exercises	*99*

A Note About The Author

Charles Dickens was born in Portsmouth in the south of England on 7th February 1812. He was one of eight children. His father, John Dickens, worked in an office as a clerk[1]. John did not earn much money in this job.

When Charles Dickens was twelve years old, his father and mother and their youngest children were all sent to prison because John could not pay their bills. Charles did not go to prison but he left school and went to work in a factory. It was a difficult job and he had to work many hours each day. Charles Dickens was very unhappy there. He never forgot how hard his life was at this time.

In 1827, when he was fifteen, Dickens went to work in a lawyer's office as a clerk. He was not paid much money but he made some friends there.

In 1833, Dickens started writing stories. He became very famous and very rich. He wrote some of the most well-known and most popular stories in English literature. During his life he wrote twenty novels and hundreds of short stories and non-fiction articles. *Oliver Twist*, the story of a poor boy without a family, was published in 1838. Other famous novels by Dickens are: *The Old Curiosity Shop* (1841), *A Christmas Carol* (1843), *Bleak House* (1853), *A Tale of Two Cities* (1859), *Great Expectations* (1861) and *Our Mutual Friend* (1865).

Charles Dickens became ill from working too hard and died on 9th June 1870. He was 58 years old. Dickens was buried in Westminster Abbey, a famous church in London.

A Note About The Story

Charles Dickens wrote this story, The Old Curiosity Shop, in 1840–1841 as part of a magazine that he published. The story was printed in 88 separate weekly parts. Later, these parts were put together and published as a book.

The parts of the story were so popular that more than one hundred thousand copies of the magazine were sold each week. Just before the last parts were published, many people sent Dickens letters begging[2] him not to end the story in a sad way. In New York people waited at the docks[3] for ships to arrive from England so that they could ask people on the ship how the story had ended. They thought that these people might have already read the last part of the story.

The Old Curiosity Shop tells the story of Nell Trent, a thirteen-year-old girl, and her grandfather, who both live at The Old Curiosity Shop in London. Nell's grandfather, who is never named in the story but is often described as 'the old man', sells curios in the shop. These are small objects that are unusual or curious (a word meaning 'interesting') that people like to collect. The curios might have included old items of furniture, pictures and things from other countries.

Nell, or 'the child' as Dickens often calls her, is an innocent, sweet girl who has a difficult life. Many of Dickens's stories are about poor children like Nell. Dickens was angry because he saw how difficult children's lives were at that time. The children were often hungry and were not well looked after. He wrote about these things because he wanted everyone to know the truth. He hoped that his stories would improve people's lives.

Charles Dickens often felt emotional about his characters when he wrote his stories. As he got near the end of this particular story, Dickens said, 'I am breaking my heart over[P] this story, and cannot bear[4] to finish it.'

England in the Nineteenth Century

The story of *The Old Curiosity Shop* takes place in London and the countryside and towns to the north of London. It is set in the first half of the nineteenth century.

In the nineteenth century, England was a very rich country and London was the largest city in Europe. Many rich people lived in London. They had expensive houses, ate the best food and wore beautiful and fashionable clothes. It was common for people with money to have servants[5] to help them in their homes. These servants were often children who were paid a small amount of money.

However, many people in England were very poor. Thousands of people in London lived in small, dirty houses and did not have enough to eat. Many people who did not have any work did not have a home and they had to beg to get enough food to live.

There were no cars, trains or telephones and travel was much slower in those days. People walked, rode horses or travelled in carriages[6] pulled by horses. When people wanted to travel long distances between towns, they paid to go in a public coach. Letters were carried in these coaches too.

There were several industrial towns, which were full of factories, in England at this time. Life in these places was often very hard, dirty and dangerous. Nell and her grandfather travel through two industrial towns on their journey. It is believed that Charles Dickens based these two places on Birmingham and Wolverhampton, which are cities in the middle of England.

The People In The Story

Nell Trent – a young girl, nearly fourteen years old; she is also sometimes called 'the child'

Nell's grandfather – an old man, the owner of The Old Curiosity Shop

Kit – Nell's friend who works at The Old Curiosity Shop; he lives with his mother and two younger brothers

Fred Trent – Nell's older brother; he is not as kind or as thoughtful as Nell

Richard Swiveller – a young man, Fred's friend; he later works as a lawyer's clerk

Daniel Quilp – a bad and frightening man; he owns a boatyard called Quilp's Wharf and lends money to Nell's grandfather

Mr Sampson Brass and Sally Brass – a brother and sister who work as lawyers; Mr Brass is Daniel Quilp's lawyer

Mr Harris and Tommy Codlin – two travelling entertainers

Mr and Mrs Garland – a kind, old couple with a son called Abel and a servant-girl called Barbara; Kit goes to work for them

Mr Marton – a kind schoolteacher; he helps Nell and her grandfather

Mrs Jarley and George – the owner of a travelling waxworks[7] and her driver

The single gentleman[8] – a man who comes to live in the same house as Mr Brass and Sally

The Marchioness[9] – Mr Brass and Sally's poor servant-girl; she becomes a good friend of Richard Swiveller

1
The Old Curiosity Shop

It was a dark, rainy night in the city of London and the light from a lamp could be seen through the front window of The Old Curiosity Shop. The room that was lit by the lamp was full of old and curious things for sale of all shapes and sizes.

In a small sitting room at the back of the building sat a man with long grey hair, whose face looked old and tired. Nearby a pretty girl with bright blue eyes was carefully preparing dinner for them both.

'Oh, Nell,' said the old man, smiling warmly at the child. 'You are such a good girl and you look after us both so well. You know that I love you, don't you, Nell?'

The child went to the old man and put her arms around him.

'Grandfather,' she replied, 'of course I know that you love me!'

The old man's face was full of worry and sadness as he spoke. 'You have spent most of your life living alone with me here and looking after me. I am sometimes afraid that you have a difficult, lonely and unhappy life.'

'Grandfather!' cried the child in surprise.

'You are poor now,' the old man continued, 'but you are a sweet and innocent girl, just like your mother was, and I won't let you be poor and die young like she did. The time is coming when you will be rich. It has been a very long time coming, but it must come at last. Yes, it must certainly come. It has come to other men who do nothing but waste[10] their lives, so why wouldn't it come to me? When *will* it come to me?'

'I am very happy as I am,' said the child, who could see that her grandfather was becoming upset.

The Old Curiosity Shop

At that moment there was a knock at the front door and Nell said cheerfully, 'Kit must have come back at last!'

The old man picked up a lit candle[11] and went to open the door. When he came back, Kit was following him. Kit was a shy boy with an unusually wide mouth, very red cheeks, a turned-up nose and untidy hair. He stopped suddenly in the doorway to the sitting room, resting himself now on one leg, then nervously moving to the other and then back again, all the while turning his old hat on his hand. Nell laughed out loud at the sight of him and Kit laughed in return.

'It was a long way I sent you, wasn't it, Kit? Did you deliver the letter to Mr Quilp?' asked the old man.

'Yes, master[12]. I did,' replied Kit.

'You must be hungry,' said the old man, and he gave Kit a slice of bread and meat and a drink. Kit went to a corner of the room and began to eat quickly.

Soon, the old man said, 'Now, Kit – it's nearly midnight. Go home, but be here on time in the morning because there's work to do. Say goodbye to him, Nell, and then get me my hat and cloak[13].'

'Goodnight, Kit,' said the child, her eyes full of happiness and kindness.

'Goodnight, Miss Nell,' replied the boy, and he left the room.

Nell helped her grandfather with his cloak and followed him to the front door. When they reached the door the old man put his arms around his granddaughter and kissed her on the forehead. A tear[14] came to Nell's eye. She hated being alone in that big, dark place all night long, not able to sleep because she was worried about her grandfather. Every night he would go out and leave her on her own, and yet he never told her where he went or what he did. Then he would return early the next day, tired, worried and sad.

'Sleep well,' he said in a low voice. 'Be safe, my sweet. I will be home early in the morning.'

The Old Curiosity Shop

The child opened the door for him to leave. The old man waited outside the door for a moment while it was closed and locked from the inside. When he was certain that the door had been locked, he walked away. At the corner of the street he stopped and looked around, perhaps to make sure that no one had seen him leaving the house, and then he disappeared into the darkness.

2
Unwanted Visitors

About a week later a young man of twenty-one years of age walked confidently into The Old Curiosity Shop. He was tall and quite handsome[15], but there was something unattractive about his clothes and the arrogant[16] way he stood.

The old man, who was alone in the shop at the time, was certainly not pleased to see him.

'Why have you come, Fred?' asked the old man. 'You are not welcome here.'

'I know,' replied Fred angrily. 'But I *am* here and I will stay until I decide it's time for me to go. I've come to see my sister.'

'Your sister!' cried the old man angrily.

'Ah! You can't change that relationship! If you could, you'd have done it years ago,' replied Fred. 'I want to see my sister, who you keep imprisoned here with all your dark secrets. You pretend to love her so that you can work her to death, and add a few shillings[17] every week to the piles of money you have hidden away. I want to see her; and I will.'

'And who are you to criticize[18] me?' cried the old man. 'Everyone knows you are a liar[19]. You've wasted everything you've ever been given and have treated your family terribly, just like your father did before he died.'

'Well, grandfather,' said the young man calmly, 'there's a friend of mine outside, and as it seems that I may have to wait some time, I'll call him in.' He stepped to the door and called out. A young man appeared and began walking slowly towards the shop. He seemed at first to be dressed fairly smartly, but when he came closer his clothes were dirty and untidy.

'This is Richard Swiveller,' said Fred, and he pulled the young man into the shop.

Unwanted Visitors

Mr Swiveller looked about him with a weak smile on his face, then winked[20] at his friend as if they shared a secret. 'Carefully, carefully, that's right,' he whispered loudly to Fred, then sat down heavily in a nearby chair.

The old man turned to his grandson and shouted, 'I suppose you want money from me. Why do you keep asking me for money? And why do you bring silly people like him here? How often do I have to tell you that I am poor?'

'And how often do I have to tell you,' replied Fred, looking coldly at him, 'that I know better?'

'You have chosen your own path in this world,' said the old man. 'Follow it. Leave Nell and me to work and lead our simple[21] life.'

'Nell will be a woman soon,' replied Fred, 'and, brought up by you, she'll forget me unless I come to see her sometimes.'

'No, of course you don't want her to forget you!' cried the old man. 'Especially when she's older and riding in an expensive carriage and she sees you poor and hungry!'

'Ah! So you admit that she will be rich when you die, do you?' replied Fred angrily. But before the old man could answer, the door opened and Nell herself appeared.

She was closely followed by a surprisingly unattractive man. He was unusually short, but his head and face were large enough for the body of a giant. His small black eyes were constantly moving; his mouth and chin were covered with a short, rough[22] beard; and his skin was of the kind that never looks clean or healthy. But what added most to the ugliness of his face was a horrible smile, which seemed to be always on his face. It showed only a few brown teeth left in his mouth. His hair was thin and long, and he wore a big, tall hat, an old, dark suit and a pair of very large shoes.

There was more than enough time to notice these details, because some moments passed before anyone spoke. Nell moved shyly towards her brother and put her hand in his. The

Unwanted Visitors

ugly little man looked carefully at the two young men, and the grandfather, who clearly had not expected this unwelcome visitor, seemed very uncomfortable.

'Ah!' said the short man, looking at Fred. 'He must be your grandson! But who is that?' he added, pointing at Richard Swiveller.

'A friend of his, but both of them are unwelcome,' said the grandfather.

'Well, Nelly,' said Fred aloud. 'Does grandfather teach you to hate me, eh?'

'No, no! Of course not,' cried the child. 'I love you dearly, Fred.' 'And if you stopped upsetting grandfather then I could love you more.'

'I see!' said Fred, and he roughly[23] kissed the child on her cheek and then pushed her away. 'That's enough then – we are friends.' He stopped speaking and followed her with his eyes until she had left the room. Then he turned to speak to the short man.

'Now, Mr …'

'Do you mean me?' said the ugly little man. 'Quilp is my name. It's easy to remember. It's not a long one – Daniel Quilp.'

'Mr Quilp, then,' continued Fred. 'You know my grandfather.'

'A little,' said Mr Quilp, quickly.

'And you know about some of his mysteries and secrets.'

'A few,' replied Quilp, simply.

'Then let me tell him once and for all[P], through you, that I will come here as often as I like, so long as he keeps Nell here. I came here today to see her, and I'll come here again fifty times for the same reason. I have seen her, and now my visit has ended.' He turned suddenly to his friend. 'Let's leave, Richard.'

'Humph!' said Quilp with a disgusted[24] look on his face when the young men had gone. 'What a selfish[25] grandson you have!' he said to the old man. 'You are such a weak man.'

'Ah!' said the short man, looking at Fred.
'He must be your grandson! But who is that?'

Unwanted Visitors

'What would you do, then?' the old man answered helplessly. Then he added, with a shake of his head, 'Something violent, I'm sure.'

'You're right there,' replied the ugly little man, who was very pleased with the comment. 'Oh yes, I like causing trouble and pain if I can!' He rubbed his hands slowly together, again and again, still with the horrible smile on his face. Then he moved very close to the old man and putting his hand into his pocket he spoke again.

'Here's the gold you asked to borrow,' he said. 'I brought it myself because it's valuable and heavy – I didn't want Nell to get into trouble carrying it on her own. But, of course, she'll soon need to get used to carrying gold, because she'll be carrying a lot when you are dead, won't she?'

'I ... I really do hope so,' said the old man quietly as he took the money.

'Hope so!' repeated Quilp, moving close to the old man's ear. 'I wish I knew what good investments[26] you are putting all my money into. But you are a private man and keep that secret well.'

'My secret!' said the old man with a worried look. 'Yes, you're right ... I ... I am quite a private man.'

When Daniel Quilp had finally left and the old man and his granddaughter were alone, he put his hand on hers and spoke.

'Don't worry, Nell,' he said gently. 'Things will get better. Yes, I'm sure ... I really hope things will get better.'

She smiled at him, but did not answer. Then there was a knock at the door. She stood up, looked at the clock and went to the door, saying excitedly, 'It must be Kit coming for his lesson!'

Nell was soon busy giving Kit a writing lesson, of which he had two every week. He found writing very hard and made many mistakes, but Nell was a patient teacher. The evening passed quickly as they laughed and chatted together and the time soon came for Kit to leave. It was not long after he had left that Nell's grandfather prepared to go out all night again. And once more the child was left alone in the darkness of The Old Curiosity Shop.

3

Fred and Richard Make a Plan

Mr Richard Swiveller lived in a small rented room above a shop in an area of London famous for its theatres and cheap houses. And it was here that Fred had come to visit him one evening. Fred had spent nearly an hour listening to Richard talking about nothing important, and he was now walking up and down the room impatiently.

'Richard,' said Fred angrily, 'I don't understand how you can be so cheerful with everything that has happened. I wish you would stop talking!'

'Well,' said Mr Swiveller, 'I must say that you are very rude! I've invited you into my fashionable gentleman's apartments and this is how you treat me! Well, I really don't know …'

'Richard!' shouted Fred, returning to his chair. 'Will you talk seriously for two minutes, if I show you a way to make a lot of money with very little effort?'

Richard Swiveller immediately fell silent and stared[27] at his friend. A moment passed before Fred spoke again.

'Do you think my sister Nell is pretty?'

'Well, yes, of course,' replied Richard. 'But I must say that you two don't look very similar at all.'

'Good – you think she's pretty,' said Fred, choosing to ignore[28] Richard's comment. 'So … it's very clear that the old man and I never agree about anything, and that he's not going to give me any money, not even when he dies. You see that, don't you?'

'A bat[29] could see that, even with the sun shining,' said Richard, nodding his head.

'Well,' Fred went on, 'Nell is a friendly girl and, because she is young, we can easily change what she thinks. You could

Fred and Richard Make a Plan

make friends with her and then she might be persuaded[30] to marry you.'

Richard Swiveller, who could not believe what he had just heard, spoke just one word.

'What!'

'She could be persuaded to marry you,' repeated Fred calmly. 'And if you married her, all that money could be yours.'

'But she's not even fourteen years old!' cried Richard.

'I don't mean you should marry her now!' replied Fred impatiently. 'I mean you could marry her in three or four years' time.'

Richard looked very uncertain.

'Look,' began Fred. 'I think I could get her to marry you. Even if the old man lived for several more years, you would inherit[31] all his money in the end. Then you and I would be able to spend it together. And just think – you would also have a beautiful wife!'

Richard thought for a moment. His rich aunt had been sending him money over the years, but in the last few months he had received nothing. She had heard about how he lived his life and wasted the money she sent him. Richard had sent her many letters asking, even begging, for money, but she refused to help him. He had always expected to inherit her money, but that would certainly never happen now. He was poor and might always be poor.

'And you are sure that he's rich?' he asked Fred.

'Am I sure? You heard what he said last week about Nell riding in an expensive carriage one day, didn't you?' replied Fred.

The conversation continued in this way. At first Richard did not think Fred's idea was a good one. However, the truth was he was poor and greedy[32], and Fred was clever and persuasive. So it was only an hour later that Richard Swiveller found himself agreeing to his friend's surprising new plan.

4
Quilp Uncovers a Secret

Mr Quilp did not have one particular job, but he did all sorts of different things for money. He collected the rent for whole areas of dirty streets near the river Thames, he lent money to sailors and he kept his eyes open[P] for new (and sometimes illegal[33]) business opportunities. He lived in Tower Hill, near the London docks, but he also had a small yard full of rats called 'Quilp's Wharf' not far away on the south side of the river Thames. It was a boatyard, but Quilp never seemed to buy or sell any boats there. He just used the old wooden building as a place to secretly keep and count all of his money.

Nell's grandfather often asked her to come to this frightening, dangerous and far-away place. He would ask her to deliver letters to Quilp. Today Nell, who was very tired and worried, had brought another of those letters. When she arrived at the boatyard the first thing she saw was Mr Quilp and the young, untidy-looking boy who worked for him. They were fighting in the yard. Quilp was shouting and then suddenly laughing loudly, and all the while he was hitting the boy hard with a large stick. At last the boy managed[34] to pull away from his ugly master for a moment. It was then that Quilp noticed Nell standing nearby.

'Oh, Nelly!' he cried.

'Yes,' said the child uncertainly.

'Come in. Don't worry about the boy,' said Quilp, walking with Nell into the counting-house.

'I've brought an important letter from my grandfather,' Nell explained and handed the ugly little man the letter. Quilp, without saying a word, opened it and began to read.

Quilp Uncovers a Secret

Quilp shook his head and said to himself, 'It's all gone already? In just twenty-four hours! What on earth[P] has he done with it? That is the mystery!'

Nell was uncomfortable and wanted to leave as soon as she could. A few moments passed during which nothing was said, but Quilp rubbed his hands together and scratched his head.

'You've brought a lot of these letters to me recently, haven't you, Nell?' Quilp said coldly. 'Have you asked your grandfather why you have to bring them?'

'Yes, I've asked him a hundred times, but he won't tell me,' replied Nell. 'It breaks my heart. He just shakes his head and looks sad.'

'But he hasn't always been such a sad old man, has he?' said Quilp unkindly.

'Oh, no!' said the child quickly. 'We were once so happy and he was so cheerful! But that has all changed since he …' and she stopped, unsure that she should tell him any more.

'Yes?' said Mr Quilp in a suddenly gentler voice. 'Since he …?'

'I … I … don't know,' replied Nell.

'Come now, Nell, you can tell me anything! In fact, I won't let you go until you tell me. So, since he …?' he repeated.

'Well, since he started going out all night, every night,' finished Nell. 'I don't know where he goes. He has no sleep or rest, apart from in his chair during the day.'

Quilp said nothing, but simply nodded his head. He wanted her to say more.

'When he comes home early in the morning,' continued the child, 'I let him in. This morning I saw that his face was white and he looked ill. And later, when he didn't know I was in the room, I heard him say that he couldn't bear his life anymore. He said, "I can't believe how unlucky I've been with the cards I've been dealt[P]." And then he said, "If I didn't have young Nell, I would wish to die." Oh! What will I do?'

Quilp Uncovers a Secret

Then the child hid her face in her hands and started to cry.

Quilp looked about him as if he was deep in thought. He stared at Nell, then reached out and put his hand heavily on her shoulder. Nell immediately stopped crying and moved quickly away from him.

'I have been away too long, sir. I have to go now,' said Nell, drying her eyes.

Mr Quilp went to his desk and started to write. Then he turned to Nell and said, 'Take this note to him. It's only to say that I will see him tomorrow, and that I couldn't do what he has asked me to do in his letter. Goodbye, Nelly.'

———

Mr Quilp waited for two days before he went to see the old man in The Old Curiosity Shop. When he went inside he found Nell's grandfather alone in the shop.

'At last!' cried the old man. 'Have you brought me any money?'

'No, never again!' answered Quilp.

'Then,' said the old man, standing up from his chair, 'Nell and I have no hope!'

'Listen to me,' said Quilp, beating his hand on the table. 'You have no secret from me now.'

The old man stared at Quilp with fear in his eyes.

'I now know what has happened to all that money I have lent you,' Quilp said. 'Every night, you've been going out with my money and gambling[35] with it, haven't you? Was that your secret plan – to make your fortune[P] by playing cards?'

'Yes!' cried the old man.

'And I thought that you were investing my money carefully in some clever business opportunity! I have been tricked by a gambler!' said Quilp, looking at him in anger.

'I'm not a gambler,' cried the old man. 'I've never played cards to make money for myself, or because I love gambling. I've only done it to try and save Nell.'

Quilp Uncovers a Secret

'So,' said Quilp, 'I suppose that you spent all your money first and then you came to me for some more. While you said you were making yourself rich, you were actually making yourself a beggar, eh? Dear me! And of course I hold every security[36] you were able to give me – including the letter which says that this building and everything in it now belongs to me.' As he said this, Quilp looked around him, as if to make sure that none of it had been taken away.

'I've had some bad luck,' said the old man. 'But with a little more money my luck will change. It *must* change! Help me, please, or at least help Nell.'

'I'm sorry, but I've got another business appointment,' said Quilp calmly, looking at his watch. 'If I hadn't unexpectedly heard about your gambling secret, perhaps I would have lent you more money. But not now.'

'Who was it that told you?' asked the old man.

Quilp simply replied, 'Who do you think it was?'

After a moment's thought the old man said, 'It was Kit. Yes, it must have been him.'

Mr Quilp said brightly, 'Yes, it was Kit. Poor Kit!' And then he turned, walked to the door and left.

5
Everything Changes

Someone, hiding in the shadows[37] across the street, had been carefully watching The Old Curiosity Shop. He had seen Daniel Quilp arrive and leave, and had noticed that the old man had not left the house that evening as usual. This person used to wait for hours and hours every night, watching the house and making sure that Nell was safe while her grandfather was gone. This kind and thoughtful person was Kit.

Sometime later, once Kit knew Nell would not be alone that night, he went home to his widowed[38] mother and his two young brothers.

'Oh Kit!' cried his mother when he walked into the small and simple room. 'I wonder what Nell would say if she knew that every night, when she is sitting all alone, you are out there on the street keeping an eye on[P] her.' She looked closely at Kit and then said, 'Some people might say you've fallen in love with her …'

Kit, whose face was starting to turn red, was saved by a loud knock at the door. It was Nell herself, looking worried and upset.

'I must not stay long,' she said. 'Grandfather is very ill.'

'I'll run to get a doctor,' said Kit, picking up his coat. 'I'll be there soon. I …'

'No, no,' cried Nell. 'The doctor is there already and … I don't know why, but grandfather's very angry with you and says you are the cause of all his problems.'

Kit looked at her with his eyes open wide.

'The doctor says you must not come near him or he will die,' added Nell, who had started to cry. 'Oh Kit, what have you done? I trusted you. You were the only friend I had!'

Everything Changes

Kit was so shocked[39] that he could not speak. Nell gave him the money that he had earned that week, and then was gone, as quickly as she had come.

———

Nell's grandfather became seriously ill and could not move from his bed. Despite[40] this, within a few days Mr Quilp closed the shop and made the house and everything in it his own. He then decided to live for a while in the back rooms of the ground floor with his lawyer – a man called Mr Sampson Brass.

Mr Brass was a tall, thin man, with an ugly nose, a large forehead, very small eyes, and hair of a deep red. He wore a very long, black coat, short, black trousers and high shoes. He was not a very pleasant[41] man and he was clearly afraid of Daniel Quilp.

'Will we be staying here long?' asked Mr Brass.

'We must stay, I suppose, until the old man upstairs is dead,' answered Quilp. 'Or, if he doesn't die quickly, we'll just tell him and his granddaughter to leave.'

'He he he!' cried Mr Brass, trying to laugh.

Nell stayed away from Quilp and his lawyer friend and spent most of the next few weeks beside her sick grandfather's bed. One night, she was sitting alone by the open window when Kit came and called to her from the street below.

'I hope you don't really believe that I've done anything wrong, Nell!' he shouted up to her. 'I can say, with a true and honest heart, that I haven't. When your grandfather gets better, will you tell him that? I want to work for him again.'

'If I did tell him, what good would it do? We are very poor now, so we wouldn't be able to pay you,' said Nell sadly.

'I don't care about the money,' replied Kit. 'I just thought … I just thought that if he believed me, then you could both come and live with my family. Just for a while. Ours is a small and simple home, but it's very clean.'

But just then Mr Brass came out and chased Kit away.

Everything Changes

Many people came to the house while her grandfather was ill, but Nell had never felt more lonely. And she knew that her grandfather would never agree to live at Kit's house. It was not long until her grandfather's illness passed. However, he was very weak. He was different now: he was confused[42] and what he said often did not make sense.

As soon as he could see that the old man was feeling a little better, Mr Quilp said that he was going to sell everything in the house and the shop. He told Nell that she and her grandfather would have to leave and find somewhere else to live.

Hearing this news, Nell began to cry and turned to her weak grandfather. 'Let's go,' she said to him. 'Let's leave this place and never come back or think of it again. We can live as beggars and be happy. I am not afraid. We can walk through the countryside and sleep in fields and under trees. In the day you can rest and I will knock on doors and beg for money. We will feel the sun and wind on our faces.'

The old man looked at his granddaughter for a few moments. There were tears in his eyes as he replied, 'Then yes, let's do that. But we must keep our plan secret. If anyone finds out, they will think I am mad and take you from me.' Then he added, 'We will be all right. You and I together, Nell, forever.'

The child's heart was suddenly full of hope. She did not think of hunger or cold or thirst or difficulties. She saw an end to their sadness and a return to the happy life they had once enjoyed together. She thought of the sun and rivers and green grass and summer days, and there were no dark corners in the picture she saw.

They left the house quietly the next morning, before Quilp and Mr Brass were awake. It was the beginning of a bright day in June, and as they stood in front of The Old Curiosity Shop Nell asked her grandfather, 'Which way should we go?'

The old man looked helplessly, first at her, then to the right and left, then at her again, and shook his head. From that moment Nell knew that she would always have to look after both of them. She took a deep breath and then held her grandfather's hand and led[43] him away.

6
The Long Journey Begins

Nell and her grandfather walked all morning through the streets of London. At first the city was quiet and peaceful in the early morning sunlight. But slowly the streets filled with people as they passed through an area with shops, and then came to streets where very poor people lived. Nell was a little afraid, but they carried on walking.

After a while she noticed that small gardens started to appear, and the rough[44]-looking houses began to turn into small cottages.

In the early afternoon they found themselves near a pleasant field and they sat down to rest and eat the bread and meat that Nell had brought. Then on they went again, walking through country roads and hearing the birds sing and the wind gently moving the branches of the trees. They walked all day, and paid some money to sleep that night at a small cottage.

Next morning they set off walking again. They often rested, but only for a few minutes at a time. It was nearly five o'clock in the afternoon when they stopped near some workmen's cottages and asked if they could buy some milk. They spent some time resting by the cottages, then continued walking to the nearest town, which was about five miles away.

The sun was setting when they reached the church in the small town. The old man led the way into the churchyard. As they walked in they heard voices and soon found two men. They were surrounded by puppets[45] lying on the ground around them.

'Are those puppets from a show?' asked the old man, excitedly. Travelling puppet shows were very popular at that time and the old man loved to watch them.

'Are those puppets from a show?' asked the old man, excitedly.

The Long Journey Begins

'Yes,' replied one of the men. 'We've come here to fix them before our show tonight. My name's Tommy Codlin and we're staying at the public house[46].'

'Good!' said the old man, reaching out to touch one of the puppets.

'Where are you travelling to?' asked the other man, whose name was Mr Harris.

'Oh, I don't think we're travelling any further tonight,' said the child, looking towards her grandfather.

'If you want a place to stop,' Harris commented, 'you should stay at the public house as well. It's very cheap.'

And so Nell and her grandfather followed the two men to the public house, where they watched the puppet performance and ate some dinner. Later, they went upstairs to their simple rooms, where the tired old man asked Nell to sit by his bed until he fell asleep.

As she sat next to him she thought of the life that was in front of them. She had a little money, but when that was gone they would have to beg. In her purse there was also one gold coin. She decided that it would be best to hide this valuable coin, and save it for a time when they really needed it. So she carefully sewed[47] the piece of gold into the bottom her dress and then, feeling a little more in control of her future, she lay down and fell into a deep sleep.

The next morning at breakfast Mr Codlin suggested that Nell and her grandfather should travel with them to the next town. Nell thought for a moment. They had no other plans and it would be good to have some company. It was agreed, and it was not long before they were all walking together down the country lane away from the public house. They walked all day, stopping only for Codlin and Harris to give short puppet shows for money in the villages they passed through.

It was raining and dark when they arrived at the next public house that they planned to stay in. A big fire was burning in

The Long Journey Begins

the kitchen. Soon both Nell and her grandfather, warm and dry at last, fell asleep near the fire, and while they were sleeping, Codlin and Harris discussed their new travelling friends.

'It's clear that the old man is mad and the young girl isn't used to this type of life,' whispered Harris. 'I think he's taken her and he's running away from someone,' he added.

'What!' cried Mr Codlin, looking worried.

Harris said quietly, 'If she's gone missing, there might be a reward[48] for her.'

Codlin, after thinking for a few moments, replied, 'You might be right. And if you are right, remember that we work together – we share everything!' Then he added, 'Yes, then we need to keep an eye on little Nell and that mad old man. We must keep them with us until we find out more information about them.'

The men did not know it, but Nell had begun to wake up and had heard Codlin's reply. The following morning Nell noticed that Codlin and Harris were watching her closely. She no longer felt safe after what she had heard them say. While the two puppeteers were busy packing up their puppets, she saw a chance to escape. Nell was afraid, but she quickly and quietly led her grandfather out through the back door of the public house. They did not stop to look behind them, but walked quickly away into the fields.

7
A New Beginning for Kit

While Nell and her grandfather were travelling through the countryside, back in London Daniel Quilp was busy making friends with Richard Swiveller. But he did not really like Richard and only wanted to play a trick on[P] him. This is what happened.

Quilp had soon discovered that Nell and the old man had left The Old Curiosity Shop. But he was not very surprised that they had gone. His only worry was that the old man might have taken some hidden money with him. Quilp did not wait. He emptied the house and shop and sold everything in it as soon as he could.

On the same day that Nell and her grandfather left London, Quilp received a visit from Richard. Richard went to the shop as part of Fred's plan to make friends with Nell and become rich. So he was shocked and upset to find that Nell, her grandfather and all the money had gone. The plan to become rich was in serious trouble before it began!

It was clear that neither Daniel Quilp nor Richard Swiveller knew where Nell and her grandfather had gone. But Quilp wanted to find out why Richard had come to The Old Curiosity Shop and so he began asking him questions. After many clever questions, Quilp learnt all about Fred's plan for Richard to marry Nell, and for Fred and Richard to make themselves rich with her large inheritance.

Quilp, however, knew more than Richard. He knew that the grandfather was really poor, not rich. But he thought it would be fun to watch Fred's plan go terribly wrong. He would laugh at them when Fred and Richard found out that Nell was a beggar!

A New Beginning for Kit

'What a clever plan!' cried Quilp unkindly. 'Oh, you lucky man! Yes, you will be Nelly's husband, with more gold and silver than you can imagine. Let's go and talk to Fred and I'll help you both find her.'

The only person who was truly sad about the disappearance was Kit. He had no idea where Nell and her grandfather were and he could not stop worrying about it. He hoped that in a few days' time they would return and accept his offer of a place to stay.

Realizing that he would never again work for Nell's grandfather at The Old Curiosity Shop, Kit started to look for another job. He walked the streets asking for work, but no one offered him any. After several days of this he was about to give up when a small carriage pulled by a stubborn[49]-looking pony[50] went past him. The driver of the carriage was a fat little old gentleman and next to him sat a fat little old lady. In the seat behind them sat a young man, who Kit thought must be their son. The old gentleman could not control the pony very well, but with difficulty he stopped the carriage in front of a house not far from Kit and the three of them climbed down from the carriage.

'Excuse me, sir,' said Kit. 'Would you like me to look after your horse?'

'If you are happy to wait for a while, yes, you can have the job,' replied the old gentleman, smiling. The family then went into the house.

Some time later they came out again and walked towards the carriage. The old gentleman put his hand in his pocket to find a sixpence for Kit. But the only coin he had was a shilling, which he thought was too much money. However, because he had no other coins, he gave the shilling to Kit.

'There,' he said with a laugh. 'I'm coming here again next Monday at the same time. Make sure that you're here, my boy, to earn the rest of this money!'

A New Beginning for Kit

'Thank you, sir,' said Kit. 'I'll be here.'

Kit meant what he said, but the three people in the carriage laughed loudly, and even the pony shook its head. Clearly none of them expected Kit to be honest and return the following Monday.

The days passed and every day Kit hoped that Nell and her grandfather would knock on his front door. They never did. Monday came again and Kit returned to the same place in the street where he had held the pony the week before. It was not long before the carriage came round the corner, sped down the street and stopped suddenly and violently as the old gentleman tried to control the pony.

It was then that Kit, with a friendly smile on his face, appeared by the pony's head.

'Look!' cried the old gentleman happily. 'The boy is here!'

'I said I would be here, sir,' said Kit, his hand on the pony's neck. 'I hope you've had a pleasant ride, sir.'

The old gentleman and his son helped the old lady out of the carriage and they went into the house. After some time they returned and the old gentleman came to speak to Kit. He said his name was Mr Garland and he asked Kit a few questions about where he lived and his family. After writing Kit's address in a small notebook, Mr Garland climbed up into the carriage with his wife and son and drove away.

It took Kit about half an hour to walk home and when he arrived he was surprised to see the pony and carriage again, standing right outside his house! Inside, Mr and Mrs Garland were there, talking to his mother in the kitchen.

'My dear,' said Kit's mother, looking at Mr Garland, who was smiling. 'This kind gentleman has offered you a job!'

After a few minutes of conversation it was decided: Kit would live in Mr and Mrs Garland's house and would be employed by them. The old couple told him that his salary would be six pounds a year.

A New Beginning for Kit

'Well, mother,' said Kit excitedly after the Garlands had left. 'Six pounds a year! We won't need to worry about money again!'

Just two days later Kit, wearing smart new clothes, arrived to start work at Mr and Mrs Garland's beautiful cottage. He knocked on the door, and after what seemed like a very long time a young servant-girl opened it. She looked shy and was very pretty.

'I suppose you're Kit, sir,' said the girl, looking down at her feet. 'My name is Barbara.'

Then she looked up at Kit, and they both smiled shyly at each other.

8
Chance Meetings

Nell and her grandfather walked for several hours before they felt that they were far enough away from the puppeteers to stop and rest. The old man was confused and frightened and did not seem to really understand what had happened. This worried and upset Nell, but she knew that she had to be strong. After a short rest they started walking again, and did not stop until they reached a village late in the afternoon.

The village was very small and they walked through it to see where they could stay. They saw an old man sitting in a little garden in front of a cottage. Nell knew that he must be the schoolteacher because above the window of the cottage was a sign that said 'School'. He wore a simple black suit and he looked friendly. Nell felt quite shy, but she went into the garden and spoke to him.

'Do you know of anywhere we could stay for the night?' asked Nell. 'We have walked a long way today and we would be happy to pay a small amount of money.'

'My name is Mr Marton,' said the schoolteacher. 'You're a very young traveller, my child. Why don't you both stay here? Come in,' he added.

It was a simple house, but Nell and her grandfather were comfortable there and had more than enough to eat and drink. They slept well, and in the morning while they were eating breakfast Mr Marton made a suggestion.

'You both look very tired,' he said. 'You're very welcome to stay here longer, before you continue with your long journey.'

And so they stayed another two nights. Nell cleaned and tidied the house during the day to show the schoolteacher how thankful she was to him. She also spent some time watching

Chance Meetings

him as he taught his class of young boys to read and write. Both she and her grandfather became friends with Mr Marton, and they were able to relax and rest in the cottage. They were a little sad when the time came for them to leave and continue with their journey.

Soon they had left the village far behind and were following the main road. They walked all day but as the sun began to set they had not found a village or town. Just as they were beginning to get worried about where they would stay, they saw a caravan at the side of the road. It seemed to be a smart little house on wheels, which was painted brightly and had white curtains at the windows. There was a woman sitting on its steps drinking a cup of tea and she looked friendly and well dressed. Just near the caravan a man – Nell guessed he was the driver – was holding two fine-looking horses that were eating the grass.

'Excuse me,' Nell said to the lady. 'Do you know how far it is to the next town? We hope to stay there tonight.'

The woman said the next town was about eight miles away.

'Oh!' cried Nell. 'That's such a long way.'

There was a moment's silence during which the woman looked carefully at both Nell and her grandfather.

'Are you hungry?' the lady asked. 'Come and have something to eat.'

And so they drank hot tea and ate bread and cheese at the side of the road. After a little more conversation, the woman invited Nell and her grandfather to ride with her in the caravan to the next town. As Nell climbed into the caravan she thanked the woman several times. She sat down inside the caravan and was happy to be saved from such a long walk so late in the day.

*'Are you hungry?' the lady asked.
'Come and have something to eat.'*

9

Nell Gets a Job

When they had started to move along the road, Nell looked round the caravan more closely. It was clean and comfortable and had a kitchen with a stove and a separate sleeping area at the back.

After a few minutes the woman reached out and picked up a large piece of paper. She put it on the floor in front of Nell.

'There, child,' she said, pointing to some large black letters at the top of the huge piece of paper.

Nell read the first words on the poster: 'Jarley's Waxworks.'

'That's me,' said the lady. 'I am Mrs Jarley.'

Then Nell read, 'Jarley's world-famous waxworks – the best collection of real waxworks in the world. One hundred life-sized wax figures!'

'Can I see the figures, ma'am[51]?' asked Nell.

'Of course,' said Mrs Jarley, smiling proudly. 'They have been taken in other vans to the town. We're going to the same town so I'm sure you'll see the collection.'

'I don't know if we will stay there long,' said the child.

'Why not?' cried Mrs Jarley. 'Where are you going?'

'We're … I don't know,' replied Nell.

'Do you mean that you're travelling about the country without knowing where you're going?' said Mrs Jarley.

'We are poor people, travelling without any plans, ma'am,' explained Nell, who was a little surprised by these sudden questions.

'Are you beggars then?' asked Mrs Jarley.

'Well,' replied the child, 'yes, I suppose we are.'

'Oh!' said Mrs Jarley. 'But you can obviously read. And probably write as well, can't you?'

Nell Gets a Job

'Yes, ma'am,' said Nell.

'Well, that's interesting,' replied Mrs Jarley, 'because I don't know how to write myself.'

They sat in silence for a few minutes while Mrs Jarley spent some time thinking. Then a few moments later she said, 'Would you like a job with me? I'd look after you well.'

'No, I can't leave my grandfather,' answered Nell, with a worried look on her face. 'What would happen to him without me? He's not well.'

Mrs Jarley had seen the way the old man sat looking into space and holding Nell's hand. She thought for a moment, then she said, 'I need you to talk to the crowds and tell them all about the waxworks. You can help me to write letters too. Your grandfather could help by looking after the figures and cleaning them. I will give you food and somewhere to sleep, and pay you as well.'

Nell was happy to accept her offer.

―――

They arrived at the edge of the town at about midnight and the driver, whose name was George, stopped the caravan next to the other waxworks vans. There was now more than enough room for them to sleep – Nell's grandfather would sleep in one of the empty vans and Nell would sleep in Mrs Jarley's comfortable caravan.

Nell had just said goodnight to her grandfather and was returning to the other caravan when she stopped and looked around her. It was a calm, quiet night and she thought that the caravans looked pretty in the moonlight. As she stood there, she saw something moving in the shadows further down the street. Suddenly, someone stepped forward. She recognized him immediately. It was the ugly, frightening Quilp!

Without a moment's thought, Nell stepped into the shadows. Luckily Quilp had not seen her and she watched him as he walked quickly down the street away from her.

Nell Gets a Job

That night Nell found it difficult to sleep. Why was Quilp in this town? Had he come here looking for them? The child felt frightened and was glad that Mrs Jarley was sleeping near her.

The next morning Nell and her grandfather helped Mrs Jarley and George to prepare the exhibition in a hall in the centre of the town. Soon everything was ready and all the wax figures were dressed and in their correct positions. Mrs Jarley then spent several hours teaching Nell the name and history of each of the wax figures so that she could tell the crowds about them later in the day.

The day went very well and lots of people paid to see the waxworks. Nell enjoyed working and felt lucky to have a job and somewhere safe to sleep. But she never stopped worrying that Quilp might still be in the town, and that he might try to take her and her grandfather away.

10
Nell has a Terrible Shock

Nell and her grandfather had been working for Mrs Jarley for several days when they were given a day to rest. In the evening they decided to go for a walk out into the countryside to enjoy the last hours of sun. It was a warm evening, but while they were walking the weather changed – the sky turned dark and storm clouds began to form above them. Soon there was very heavy rain and strong winds, so they ran inside a nearby public house.

'Welcome to my pub!' said the landlord cheerfully.

As they stood drying themselves by the fire, Nell heard men's voices coming through an open door. Her grandfather moved closer to her and whispered excitedly, 'They're playing cards in the next room! Don't you hear them?'

Her grandfather was right. Nell could hear the men discussing the game and how much money they had already won or lost. She looked at her grandfather and was worried to see he had changed: his eyes were now wide open, his face was quite red and he was breathing quickly.

'Oh Nell,' he said happily. 'This is it! I've always known that my chance would come to win a lot of money! I've always dreamt of this moment! How much money have we got, Nell? I saw you with some money yesterday. Give it to me now.'

'No, let me keep it, grandfather,' said the frightened child. 'Let's go from here. I don't want to stay.'

'Give me the money!' ordered the old man angrily.

'Please don't take it,' said the child, beginning to cry.

'Don't cry, Nell,' said her grandfather. 'I didn't mean to upset you. I only want to do this for you, to look after you! Now, give me the money. I must have it.'

Nell has a Terrible Shock

Nell took a little purse out of her pocket. He grabbed[52] it, turned and walked quickly into the other room. Nell followed slowly. There were two rough-looking men sitting with cards and silver coins on the table between them. One of the men, who was much bigger than the other, looked up when they came into the room.

It took a few minutes for Nell's grandfather to persuade the men to let him play, but at last he sat down at the table with them. The landlord also sat down and the four men began to play a new game of cards.

The child sat near them and watched how at one moment her grandfather shouted with excitement and at the next moment looked terribly sad and upset, then happy again. It was the first time she had seen him like this and it frightened her. She now understood that he could not stop himself and that he had a serious problem with gambling.

After what seemed like hours, the card game came to an end. The large man had won, and Nell's purse lay completely empty in front of her grandfather. For a few moments the old man stayed at the table looking again and again at the cards that lay there. Nell walked to him and put her hand on his shoulder.

'If the game had gone on just a little longer, I think I would have won!' he said.

Nell said nothing. It was now very late and the storm was still blowing outside. Her purse was empty, but Nell remembered that she still had that one gold coin which she had sewn into the bottom of her dress. She told her grandfather about the coin and suggested that they stay the night at the pub. Nell used the gold coin to pay the landlord. He was surprised to see such a valuable coin and he gave her back some smaller coins before showing them to their rooms upstairs.

Later, Nell did not feel comfortable when she was alone in her room. It was a large, dark house and it took her a long

Nell has a Terrible Shock

time to fall asleep. When she did finally sleep her head was full of terrible dreams. Then suddenly she woke up. It was dark, but she could see a shadowy figure standing in her room! She wanted to cry out, but she was too frightened to move or make a sound. The terrible figure slowly moved around her bed and it began searching for something. After a few moments she watched it leave the room. She was shocked to see the figure then go silently to her grandfather's door and inside his room! She could not bear it any longer. As quietly as she could, she climbed out of bed and went to the open door of his room.

What she saw in front of her was terrible. The bed had not been slept in, and sitting at a small candlelit table was her grandfather. His head was down and he was counting the money which he had just stolen from his own granddaughter.

Nell had been frightened, but now she felt sick. She could not believe what she saw. She felt that she did not know the man who was her grandfather. Silently, she returned to her room and lay awake worrying until morning.

The next day, as they were walking back to the caravans, Nell told her grandfather that someone had stolen her money during the night. Her last hope disappeared when she heard her grandfather's reply.

'But don't we have any more money?' he asked. 'Then we must get some more.'

That night, when he thought Nell was fast asleep, the old man left his van. But Nell was not asleep, and when he came back hours later, she saw that he was sad because he had lost all the money gambling again.

'Get me more money,' he ordered. 'I'll make you rich. Just get me some more money.'

What could Nell do? Her grandfather was not well. In the next few days she gave him all the money she earned. It upset her to do this, but she was worried that he would steal money from Mrs Jarley if she did not.

*Nell had been frightened, but now she felt sick.
She could not believe what she saw.*

11
Richard Gets a Job

The simple and cheap office of Mr Sampson Brass (who you might remember was Quilp's lawyer) was in a narrow street somewhere in London. There was a sign on the door that said, 'Mr Sampson Brass, Lawyer,' and another sign in the window which read, 'First-floor room available to rent to a single gentleman.'

Miss Sally Brass, the lawyer's sister, also spent her life working in this office. She was a lady of about thirty-five, who was very tall and thin and looked almost exactly the same as her brother. She had the same red hair and the same ugly nose. Her voice was deep and serious, and once you heard it you never forgot it. She was serious and hard-working and took pleasure in annoying her brother. It was a surprise, with all these attractive qualities, that no man had ever asked to marry her. Instead, she had spent her life studying law.

'Why do we need a clerk?' Miss Sally Brass asked her brother that morning. 'I've always helped you in the office, so why do we need one now?'

'Because Mr Quilp tells me I need one,' he replied. 'Mr Quilp is our biggest client[53]. Nearly all of our work comes from him. He has told me that this Mr Swiveller, a friend of his, is perfect for the job of clerk, so what can I do? If we say no, we'll lose all our work.'

Miss Sally did not reply, but looked coldly at him and went on with her work.

A while later there was a knock at the front door. But before Mr Brass could stand up, the door opened and in walked Mr Quilp himself, with Richard Swiveller behind him, looking uncomfortable.

Richard Gets a Job

'Here he is,' said Quilp, 'my dear friend Mr Richard Swiveller. He is from a good family and I'm sure in the end he'll inherit a lot of money. But he's young and he hasn't made very good decisions. So he is happy to accept your very kind offer of a job here as your clerk. He can start today.'

Mr Brass did not remember making the kind offer that Quilp had just mentioned. However, he stood up, put a smile on his face, shook hands with the new gentleman and then said goodbye to Quilp.

Mr Richard Swiveller was given a seat and was asked to copy out a document. About an hour later Mr Brass and Sally told him that they were going out. If anybody came to the office, they explained, he should tell them to come back later.

Richard stopped working the minute the pair had gone. He sat back and relaxed in his chair. Not long after, there was a knock at the front door. At first he did not answer it, but the person knocked again and again. Then he heard feet on the stairs. When it was clear that the knocking was not going to stop, Richard stood up and went into the hallway, where a very small, thin girl was standing at the top of the cellar[54] steps.

'Who are you?' asked Richard in surprise.

The girl, who looked dirty and frightened, did not answer the question but said, 'Oh please, sir. Will you open the door and show him the room for rent?'

'I don't know anything about the room,' said Richard. 'Why don't you show him yourself?'

'Miss Sally said I wasn't allowed to. It's eighteen shillings a week and I cook and wash the clothes,' she said quietly and quickly.

'What?' cried Richard. 'You mean that *you* are the cook?'

The girl disappeared down the stairs, so Richard opened the front door. A bald, well-dressed gentleman stood there.

'I see that you have a room for a single gentleman to rent,' he said, pointing to the sign in the window. He walked past

Richard Gets a Job

Richard and up the stairs, asking as he went, 'How much does it cost?'

Richard, thinking quickly, decided to try his luck[P] and ask for a higher rent. 'It's one pound a week, sir. And you will need to pay two weeks' rent in advance[P].'

'I'll take it,' replied the gentleman when he had seen the room. 'But I'll stay for more than two weeks. I will be here for two years. Here, I'll pay you ten pounds right now. I'm quite a private person and I don't want to be disturbed. I want to come and go when I want to, sleep when I want to.' He was certainly an unusual man.

When Mr Brass returned home he was delighted to hear about the new lodger[55] and how much he had agreed to pay.

12
The Single Gentleman

The single gentleman renting the room refused to tell anyone his name. He never spoke to Mr Brass or Sally, came and went at unusual times, and sometimes slept all day. The only thing he seemed to be interested in was travelling puppet shows. For several weeks he went to all of the shows that passed through that area of London and he became friends with many of the puppeteers. He would often invite them back to his room for a drink after the show. One day he met the puppeteers Tommy Codlin and Mr Harris. While they were talking he asked them whether they had ever met a young girl called Nell and her grandfather. He had asked the same question to all the other puppeteers he had met .

'Yes! We saw them both,' cried Mr Harris, who then turned to his friend. 'See, Tommy – I told you someone would be looking for those two.'

'Do you know where they are now?' asked the single gentleman quickly.

'One of our friends said he saw them. They were travelling with a waxworks,' said Tommy.

'If you can find out exactly where they are,' the single gentleman told them, 'I'll give you both some money. Find out and then come back to me.'

―――――

Meanwhile Kit had been getting to know Mr and Mrs Garland, their son Abel, Barbara and Whisker the pony. Whisker was difficult at first, but the people were pleasant and Kit was happy in his new job. And soon Whisker grew to love him.

One morning a smartly dressed stranger arrived and asked if he could speak to Kit. The stranger was the single gentleman.

The Single Gentleman

'I've been abroad for many years,' he told Kit. 'I've come back to London looking for something dear to my heart and I hoped to find it at The Old Curiosity Shop. But the shop is now closed and everyone has gone. I was told you might know where the old man who owned it is. Do you know?'

Over the next few minutes Kit told the single gentleman everything that had happened, ending his story with Nell and her grandfather's disappearance. Kit told him he had no idea where they were now. 'But there's a sign on the shop door,' Kit added. 'It says that all enquiries[56] should be made to Mr Sampson Brass, Mr Quilp's lawyer.'

'Yes, I know,' said the single gentleman. 'I saw the sign too and I've even rented a room in Mr Brass's house to try and find out more information. But I've learnt nothing.'

There was a moment's silence and then he said, 'I'll leave you now,' and he put a coin into Kit's hand. 'Please don't tell anyone about this meeting.'

Kit followed the single gentleman out into the street to say goodbye. And at that same moment Mr Richard Swiveller was walking down the same street and he saw Kit saying goodbye to his visitor. Richard was very surprised to see the single gentleman, Mr Brass's lodger, talking to Kit, the boy who used to work at The Old Curiosity Shop. Why on earth would these two be together? After the single gentleman had gone, Richard went over to Kit and asked him, but Kit seemed to know nothing about the man, not even his name.

The very next day a note came for Kit from the single gentleman. In the note he asked Kit to go and work for him for a while and help him to find Nell and her grandfather. He would pay Kit extra to do this. Mr Garland said that this would be all right, so Kit agreed to help the single gentleman. A carriage was sent to collect him straightaway.

He arrived at the single gentleman's lodgings and was welcomed inside. The man did not wait to tell Kit the

The Single Gentleman

latest news. 'I think I have found your old master and his granddaughter,' he began. 'I've just heard that they are in a town six hours' carriage ride from here. The old man might not remember me, but he and Nell know you. They wouldn't be frightened if you were there. Will you come with me?'

'I'm afraid that won't work,' replied Kit sadly. 'Nell told me that her grandfather never wanted to see me again.'

'Oh,' replied the single gentleman. 'Isn't there anyone else they know and would trust?'

Kit thought for a moment and then he answered, 'Well, the only person I can think of is my mother. She cares about Nell as much as I do.'

After a few minutes of planning, Kit went to talk to his mother. He explained that the single gentleman wanted her to travel with him to look for Nell and her grandfather. Kit helped his mother pack a few things for the journey and then he asked a neighbour to look after his little brothers while their mother was away.

Soon Kit's mother and the single gentleman were in a carriage and on their way. Kit stood at the side of the road and watched them go with tears in his eyes. They were not tears of sadness, but tears of joy at the thought of seeing Nell again, beautiful, sweet Nell.

13
Nell is Given Hope

Poor Nell did not know what to do. Her grandfather was taking all her money and gambling it away with other travellers every night. She knew this because she had secretly followed him to find out where he was going. One night, while standing in the shadows, she had heard the men he gambled with asking him for more money. When he said that he had no more money, one of the men made a terrible suggestion.

'What about that waxworks woman you work for?' the man began. 'She makes a lot of money and I've heard she keeps it in a metal box under her bed at night. She doesn't lock her door because she's afraid of fire. Go in there when she's asleep and take the money. Anyone could go in there and do it, so she won't know it's you. It will be easy!'

They talked about it for some time until the grandfather finally agreed that he would steal all of Mrs Jarley's money and return the next night.

What could Nell do? She could not let him steal money from Mrs Jarley. So later that night she woke up her grandfather and told him that they had to leave. She packed up their things and took him away from the caravans while Mrs Jarley and George were still sleeping. She led him by the hand to the top of a nearby hill and there they rested. Nell started to cry. Then later that night they lay down and slept on the grass.

It was a long way to the next town and they travelled slowly through the countryside for the next day and night. At last they walked into the town, which was very noisy and full of factories. It was raining hard now and Nell was tired, cold and wet. She had started to feel ill and they had very little money. She did not like the town. They spent several hours walking

Nell is Given Hope

through the busy streets without knowing what to do or where they would stay that night. Evening came and Nell found a dry doorway where they could lie down to sleep.

In the morning Nell and her grandfather started to walk towards the countryside again. They walked all day through ugly, dirty streets where poor, thin people worked. As day turned to night, the factories seemed to be dangerous, frightening places. They saw sick, hungry people who were crying in the street and children who were homeless. By now, Nell was very ill and she became weaker and weaker. All they had eaten that day was some bread. She could not walk anymore so she lay down at the side of the road to sleep.

The next morning they carried on, with slow, tired steps. They had nothing to eat and as evening came Nell felt again that she could not walk another step. She saw another traveller ahead of them on the road and called out to him, hoping that he might give them some food. The man turned and, as he walked towards her, Nell suddenly screamed and fell to the ground in shock. It was Mr Marton, the schoolteacher! He picked her up in his arms and carried her as fast as he could to a nearby public house.

'She is very ill and weak,' he told her grandfather, who was very worried about her.

The landlady of the pub ran to Nell and gave her some medicine and a drink. Then Nell was taken to a bed upstairs, where she slept for several hours. The next morning she woke up feeling a little better and was able to eat something. Mr Marton kindly paid for all three of them to stay another night at the public house so that Nell could rest.

'Thank you so much,' Nell said to the schoolteacher. 'If we hadn't met you, I think I might have died. I don't know how I can thank you for your help and for paying for us to stay here.'

'That's enough talk about dying!' answered Mr Marton. 'And the money is no problem. Since the last time I saw you, I have been given another job. I am going to be clerk and schoolteacher in a village several days' journey from here. That is where I am travelling to now. They are going to pay me thirty-five pounds a year!'

'I'm very happy for you,' replied Nell.

Mr Marton said that he thought of Nell as a good friend and suggested that she and her grandfather should come with him to his new village. 'I'm sure you would find a job there,' he told her.

And so they agreed that the next day he, Nell and her grandfather would travel together by public coach to the village.

14
Quilp Makes a Plan

Now we must return to Kit's mother and her journey with the single gentleman. It was not a relaxed journey. Kit's mother spent the whole time worrying about her two young children, whom she had left behind. The single gentleman spent his time worrying about finding Nell and her grandfather. They travelled all night at speed, stopping only to eat dinner. Then Kit's mother fell asleep in the carriage and was woken in the morning as the carriage came to a stop.

'This is the place!' cried the single gentleman. He climbed out of the carriage and, after asking a few people in the street, he found the hall with the waxworks. But it did not take long for him to find out from Mrs Jarley that Nell and her grandfather were no longer there. Mrs Jarley explained how she had met Nell and her grandfather, and how she had given them each a job and a place to live. Then she told him that they had suddenly disappeared. She said that she was very worried about them because the old man had seemed unwell and confused. She had tried to find them, but had had no luck.

The single gentleman was very upset at this news and said he did not know where to look next. He took Kit's mother to a nearby public house where they could stay the night. As they went up to their rooms, Kit's mother was amazed to see Mr Quilp coming down the stairs.

She stepped backwards in surprise and cried, 'Goodness me!'

'Kit's mother!' said Quilp and he smiled his horrible smile at her.

'Mr Quilp,' said the single gentleman. 'We have met before. You may remember that the day I arrived in London, I found

Quilp Makes a Plan

The Old Curiosity Shop empty and closed up. A neighbour told me to come and see you. I discovered that you had taken that shop and everything in it. And you had forced the old man who used to live there to leave and become a beggar.'

'That shop legally belongs to me,' replied Quilp. 'I didn't force him, he went by his own choice – he disappeared in the night.'

'You didn't help me when I came to you, and now you are following me. Why?' asked the single gentleman with anger in his voice.

'Following you!' cried Quilp. 'I'm not following you!'

The single gentleman simply looked at Quilp. There was nothing more to say.

Quilp returned to his room upstairs and thought for a long time about what had happened in the last few days. He had been to the office of his lawyer friend Mr Brass and had spoken to Richard Swiveller there. Richard had talked about the single gentleman who was staying in Mr Brass's house – the same gentleman who had come to see Quilp some weeks before. Richard had also said that on another day he had seen the single gentleman and Kit talking together. Wasn't that a strange thing?

Quilp had guessed from all this that the single gentleman was trying to find Nell and her grandfather. Quilp wanted to know why, so he decided to go and see Kit's mother. He thought it would be easy to frighten her and she would tell him everything she knew.

But when he got there he saw her getting into the carriage with the single gentleman, about to start their journey. He talked to the driver, found out exactly where the carriage was going, and followed it in a public coach. And now they had all met in this public house.

'So,' Quilp said quietly to himself, 'that horrible boy Kit keeps getting in my way[P]. It's Kit and his mother who are

Quilp Makes a Plan

helping to find Nelly now and will end up being rewarded. So I think I will have to kill him. Yes, that single gentleman would have paid me a lot of money to find Nell and her grandfather if Kit hadn't got in the way!'

The next morning Quilp caught the public coach back to London. As soon as he got there he went to see Mr Brass and Sally. He told them about Kit, how he kept getting in the way and how he hated him. Mr Brass, who did not really know Kit at all, said that he completely agreed with Quilp.

'You are my good friends, aren't you?' said Quilp.

'Yes! Yes, of course,' replied Mr Brass, nodding his head several times.

'Then find a way to get rid of[57] Kit. I hate him. Do you understand me?' said Quilp coldly. 'Let's shake hands on it[P].'

Mr Brass and Sally looked at each other and then both shook hands with Quilp.

15
A Village Life

When Mr Marton, Nell and her grandfather arrived at the village, Mr Marton went to get the keys to his new house. Nell and the old man waited near the church. When Mr Marton returned, he had a surprise for his travelling friends.

'Do you see that house there?' he asked, pointing to a very old but pretty house nearby. Nell nodded.

'Well,' he continued, 'it is yours for as many years as you want it.'

'Ours!' cried the child.

'Yes,' replied Mr Marton happily. 'There are two houses and I will be living in the house next door to that one.'

He then explained to Nell a little more about the house. The woman who had lived there used to look after the church keys. Her job had been to open and close the church and show it to visitors. She had died a few weeks before and a new person was now needed to do this job and live in the house. Nell could be that person! It was like her job with the waxworks.

'I've spoken to the clergyman[58]. The job would give you some money,' said Mr Marton. 'It wouldn't be very much, but enough money to live on in this simple place.'

'Thank you so much!' cried the child.

For the next two days they cleaned and prepared the houses. Nell still did not feel well but she did her best to work hard. Some of the local people came to welcome them, to offer their help or to bring some food.

Nell was given the keys to the church. She spent some time on her own, walking slowly around it. At first she felt happy and calm to be in the beautiful church, but seeing all the graves[59] in the graveyard made her feel sad because many of them were where children had been buried. She sat down near one of these graves and started to cry.

Mr Marton, walking past, saw her. 'Nell, what's wrong?' he asked her.

'It makes me so sad that these children who have died are forgotten so quickly,' she answered.

'No, no,' disagreed her friend. 'No one who dies is forgotten. Perhaps there are no flowers on these graves now, but these people are not forgotten. All of the good things they did will live on in the hearts of the people who knew them.'

Nell smiled a little, but she looked tired and her skin seemed white in the sunlight.

The next day Nell started to tidy up the graveyard and plant flowers on some of the graves. She worked all day there and her grandfather helped her. Later in the afternoon Mr Marton came and watched her working. At first he smiled because she had started to make the graves look cared for and bright. But then his heart became heavy and he sat in silence when he realized that Nell had only worked on the graves of children. Her grandfather had noticed the same thing. He stood for a moment with a worried look on his face and then moved towards Nell and put his hand gently on her shoulder. He told her how she was growing stronger and stronger each day and would soon become a woman.

The weeks passed and the new village began to feel like home. But Nell still seemed tired and ill and spent a lot of time sitting quietly looking into the fire. Both her grandfather and Mr Marton were very worried about her.

16
There are Problems for Kit

Back in London, Richard Swiveller was alone in Mr Brass's office, relaxing in a chair. There was a knock at the door and when he opened it he saw Kit standing there.

'Is your lodger at home?' asked Kit. 'I have a letter for him from Mr Garland.'

Not long after this Mr Brass and Sally returned. When they heard that Kit was upstairs visiting the single gentleman, Mr Brass immediately sent Richard out to deliver a letter. Mr Brass and his sister whispered for a few moments and then Sally went to the kitchen. Mr Brass sat alone in the office with the door open and waited for Kit to come downstairs.

Kit, after quite some time, came downstairs and Mr Brass called out to him.

'Kit,' he called, 'could you come in here before you go?'

Kit shyly stepped into the room.

'Oh dear!' said Mr Brass. 'The last time we saw each other was when Mr Quilp made The Old Curiosity Shop and everything in it his own. What must you think of me? But, Kit, that was a painful[60] job for me!'

Kit did not know what to say so he stayed silent.

'The only good thing in my job, Kit,' added Mr Brass the lawyer, 'is that at least I can help the people who are hurt when something like that happens. I want you to know that I tried to stop Quilp,' he continued. 'I begged him to let the child and her grandfather stay for a few days in the house. And I saw enough while I was there,' said Mr Brass, 'to know that you are a good person with a good heart.'

Mr Brass doesn't seem a bad person after all, thought honest Kit.

There are Problems for Kit

'Anyway,' said Mr Sampson Brass, pointing to two half crowns on the desk. 'I want you to take these.'

Kit looked at the coins and then at Mr Brass.

'They are from the lodger upstairs,' said Brass. 'But he's a very private man, so it's best if you don't tell anyone. Or say they are from me if you want to. Take them. And I don't think these will be the last coins he will give you. Goodbye, Kit. Goodbye!'

Kit took the money, thanked Mr Brass many times and left the office. A moment later, Sally appeared.

'So,' said Sally, 'did it go all right?'

'Oh yes,' replied Mr Brass with a smile. 'It went very well. Kit comes here at least once a week, so I will call him into the office the next time he comes too.'

———

When Richard Swiveller was in the office and not out delivering important messages, he was often alone. He was a lazy man and would play cards on his own rather than do any work. One day, as he was playing cards, he heard someone moving just outside the office door. He saw it was the thin servant-girl, who had been watching him through the keyhole in the door.

'Why don't you come in here and I'll teach you to play cards?' said Richard.

'Miss Sally would kill me if she knew I'd come upstairs!' cried the girl.

'Then I'll come downstairs,' he replied brightly. 'She won't kill *me*!'

He followed the girl down to the cellar, then got her some bread and meat from the kitchen. When he gave her the food she ate it faster than he had ever seen anyone eat before.

'How old are you?' he asked the girl.

'I don't know,' came the reply.

'Well, what's your name?' Richard asked.

'I don't know,' she repeated.

There are Problems for Kit

'Oh,' said Richard, a little shocked. 'Then I will call you the Marchioness.'

Richard taught her to play cards and they played until it was time for Richard to go home. After that, they secretly played cards together many times and they became good friends.

A couple of weeks later, Sally Brass told Richard that she was worried about something. She asked him if he had seen a silver pencil-case. He replied that he had not.

'It has disappeared,' Sally said, 'and I think someone has stolen it. Other things have gone missing too. Four half crowns have disappeared as well.'

Oh, thought Richard, *I hope it isn't anything to do with the Marchioness!*

Mr Brass then entered the office carrying a five-pound note, which he was holding up and looking at carefully.

'I was just telling Mr Swiveller that we think things have been stolen from the office,' Sally said to her brother.

'Ah, yes,' agreed Mr Brass sadly, as he put the bank note down on his desk and walked to the chair.

'Oh, don't leave that note there!' cried Richard.

'No, sir,' replied Mr Brass calmly. 'I *am* going to leave it there. I trust you, and I want you to know that.'

Some moments passed while they all quietly thought about the missing things. Then Sally cried, 'I've got it! It must be that boy Kit! He has come here a lot recently and is often here when we are out!'

'No!' cried Mr Brass, a look of surprise on his face. 'I can't believe it! Kit is such an honest boy.'

Then, strangely, there came a knock at the door and Kit himself walked into the house and went upstairs to see the single gentleman.

Immediately, Mr Brass sent Richard away to take a letter across town. And Sally went to the kitchen. When Kit came back downstairs, Brass called him into his office.

There are Problems for Kit

'Come on in, Kit. Put your hat down there,' said Mr Brass.

Kit put his hat down on the desk and they talked for a few minutes about Mr Garland and his family. As they talked, Mr Brass picked up the hat and moved it several times around the desk. The desk was covered in papers and it seemed that Mr Brass was looking for something.

Then, quite suddenly, Mr Brass said, 'Oh, I need to go upstairs for a minute to check something. Would you mind keeping an eye on the office for me while I'm gone?' And he disappeared upstairs for ten or more minutes.

When he came back down, both Richard and Sally had returned to the office, but Kit had gone.

'Did you let Kit look after the office on his own?' Sally asked her brother.

'Yes, I did. Despite what you say, I trust Kit,' Mr Brass replied. Then he started to move the papers around on his desk as if he was looking for something. 'Oh dear. Where's the …?' he started.

'What have you lost?' asked Richard.

'The five-pound note. I put it on my desk, but it's gone!' Mr Brass said.

'There! I told you it was him!' said Sally.

'But you don't think Kit took it, do you?' said Richard.

'Yes!' cried Sally. 'Go after him!'

Richard and Mr Brass ran out into the street and some minutes later they returned with Kit between them, each of the men holding one of Kit's arms. Kit looked shocked when they told him what they thought he had done. He agreed that they could check his pockets.

'But you won't find anything,' Kit said.

Mr Brass carefully looked through all of Kit's clothing but found nothing. Then he told Richard to check Kit's hat. At first Richard found only a handkerchief, but then, suddenly, he was holding a five-pound note in his hand.

There are Problems for Kit

'What? It was in his hat!' cried Mr Brass, acting surprised. 'Oh dear, I don't believe it! And I trusted him so much. I am a lawyer, so I must follow the law. Richard, please can you go and find a policeman?'

Mr Brass and Sally held Kit tightly while they waited for Richard and the policeman to return. When the policeman arrived, a statement[61] was taken and then a carriage was called to take Kit to be seen by a magistrate[62].

'I am not guilty!' cried Kit when the carriage arrived to take him away. 'Mr Brass, you know I am honest. Anyone who knows me can see I am honest! Do one thing for me, all of you. Please take me to Mr Garland before you take me to the magistrate.'

And so Kit was taken to see Mr Garland. Both Mr Garland and his son Abel were shocked when they heard about the five-pound note.

'I don't believe one word of this,' said Mr Garland.

'Have you noticed that Kit has had more money than usual?' asked the policeman.

'Well, yes,' replied Mr Garland. 'But Kit told me that Mr Brass himself had given him some money recently.'

'That's right, isn't it, Mr Brass?' said Kit. 'You gave me the half crowns from the single gentleman.'

'Eh?' replied Mr Brass, with a confused look on his face. 'Oh dear, this is bad. This is too much,' he added, shaking his head.

'What!' cried Kit. 'Are you saying that you didn't give me any money?'

'Give you money?' said Mr Brass. 'Of course I never did.'

'Gentlemen,' cried Kit, 'he did it! I don't know what I have done to upset him, but he must have hidden the note in my hat himself. Look at him – he is changing colour and going red. Who looks the most guilty – he or I?'

'Well, we will let the magistrate decide who is telling the truth here,' said the policeman.

*'What? It was in his hat!' cried Mr Brass, acting surprised.
'Oh dear, I don't believe it! And I trusted him so much.'*

There are Problems for Kit

And then Kit was taken from Mr Garland's house to the justice-room[63]. It seemed that there was no hope. A prison officer told Kit that he would be found guilty and would probably be sentenced to prison and transported to a far-away country. Kit spent a terrible night locked up, waiting for his future to be decided.

17
There is Hope for Kit

Several evenings later Daniel Quilp asked Sampson Brass to come and see him at his boatyard. Mr Brass hated going to that place – it was far away, dark and dangerous. When he reached the boatyard, Mr Brass knocked on the counting-house door and walked inside. After some moments of conversation Quilp told Mr Brass why he had asked to see him.

'I told you to get a clerk and you did,' he began. 'Now I'm telling you to get rid of him.'

'What?' said Mr Brass in surprise.

'I brought Richard Swiveller to you so that I could know where he was and what he was doing,' replied Quilp. 'He wanted to marry Nell because he thought her grandfather was rich, but I thought he was as poor as a rat. That marriage would have been something to see! But if the lodger is looking for the old man, then he can't really be poor, can he? So there would be no fun in helping Richard to marry Nell, none at all.'

'Oh,' replied Mr Brass.

'And his friend, Fred Trent, has disappeared,' said Quilp. 'I've heard that he had to run away because he got into trouble. I think he's gone abroad. I hate him, so that's the best place for him – far away.'

'Yes, of course!' agreed Brass.

'Swiveller is stupid and weak and I don't want him any longer,' Quilp told Brass. 'Do what you like with him – kill him or let him die of hunger, I don't care. But as soon as Kit's trial[64] is finished, get rid of Richard.'

A few days later, Kit's trial was held. The trial did not go well for Kit and he was found guilty. Kit was shocked, and his mother was very upset and could not stop crying. Richard

There is Hope for Kit

Sviveller kindly took her home, then he returned to Mr Brass's office. He was beginning to think that perhaps Kit was innocent.

But Richard had some bad news of his own when he arrived at the lawyer's office. His boss told him that he was no longer needed there and that he should look for work somewhere else. Richard was shocked and angry. He picked up his things and left without saying goodbye.

The last few days had been difficult for Richard Swiveller. That night he became very ill with a high temperature. He went home and went to bed and fell into a terrible half-sleep during which he did not know what time or day it was.

When at last he started to feel a little better, he realized that there was someone in the room with him. As he slowly opened his eyes, he saw the Marchioness. *Yes, it is her*, he thought, *sitting at my table playing cards by herself!* When she saw him looking at her she started to cry with joy.

Richard had been very ill for nearly three weeks. When the Marchioness had heard that he was ill – the only person who had ever been nice to her – she had run away from Mr Brass and Sally. She had stayed at Richard's apartment and looked after him.

She told him that Kit had been sentenced to transportation, and that she felt terrible about it because she knew he was not guilty. She said she had heard Mr Brass and Sally talking about Kit and about how Daniel Quilp had asked them to get rid of the boy. She had also heard them planning to hide the five-pound note in Kit's hat.

When the Marchioness had finished talking, Richard was very upset and angry about what he had just heard. Kit really was innocent! Richard was too weak to get out of bed so he sent the Marchioness to go and bring Mr Garland at once.

18
Quilp's Luck Changes

When Richard woke up the following morning, he could hear quiet voices in his room. Mr Garland, his son Abel, the single gentleman and the Marchioness were all there. Before he ate his breakfast, he asked Mr Garland an important question.

'Is it too late to save Kit?' he asked.

'No, I don't think so,' replied Mr Garland. 'With the information we have, we think we might be able to save him. But we are not sure that there is enough information to put Quilp, who is the real criminal, in prison.'

'Oh,' said Richard. 'But there must be a way of catching him.'

'Well, we hope that we can get Sally Brass to admit to what she has done. That might give us the information and proof[65] that we need,' explained the single gentleman. 'When she finds out how much we know, and how we know it,' he continued, 'she will realize that she's in serious trouble. And she might want to tell us about her brother and Quilp.'

They decided to send a message asking Sally to come and meet an 'unknown friend' as soon as possible at a nearby coffee-house. It was only an hour or two later that Sally appeared at the coffee-house. She was shocked to see Mr Garland and her lodger waiting there for her.

'Miss Brass,' started Mr Garland, 'we have found your missing servant-girl.'

'Have you?' she said coldly. 'That girl is trouble.'

Mr Garland explained in detail what the Marchioness had told them – what she had heard Mr Brass and Sally saying about Kit. When they had finished talking, Sally said nothing.

Quilp's Luck Changes

'So,' Mr Garland then said, 'I think you know the trouble you and your brother are in. But Quilp is a much more serious criminal than either of you. If you help us to catch him, it will make your crime look smaller.'

Hearing this, Sally Brass said nothing but thought carefully. At that moment her brother, Sampson Brass, appeared. He explained that he had followed his sister and had been listening to the whole conversation. He looked terrible and had cuts on his face.

'Look at me,' he said. 'Who do you think did this to me? Yes, Daniel Quilp. He is my client and I try to please him, but he has treated me like a dog. Some of the truth is out now, and I'm going to tell you everything. I want to get him, before he gets me.' Then, very quickly, Mr Brass told the whole story from start to finish. When he had ended his story, the men told him to write it down on paper. They said he would have to be sent to trial, too.

Sally Brass was very angry that her brother had told them everything so quickly and easily, but there was nothing she could do. Later that evening, the written statement was taken to the justice-house. They were told that a warrant for Quilp's arrest[66] would be prepared the next day and that Kit would be freed very soon.

Mr Garland and the single gentleman returned to Richard's apartment to tell him the good news. He and the Marchioness were very happy to hear that Quilp would be arrested and Kit would be freed.

The next morning, Richard received a letter from a lawyer. He did not know what this letter would say, but he opened it. He was shocked when he read it. In the letter it read that his rich aunt had died and that she had left him one hundred and fifty pounds a year. It was not the large inheritance that he had hoped for but it would be enough for him to live a comfortable, if simple, life.

'What a letter!' said Richard to himself, laughing and crying at the same time. 'I will use this money to look after the Marchioness and make a lady of her!' he promised.

Quilp, who had not left his counting-house for several days, also received a letter. When he opened it he saw that the letter was from Sally Brass. This is what the letter said:

Sampson has told several people exactly what has happened. They know everything. Some strangers are coming to catch you. You must run away quickly. I have disappeared and you should, too.

Quilp was shocked and angry. He decided that he would leave the boatyard that night while it was dark. He closed up the counting-house and pushed a few things that he might need into his pockets. As he did this he talked to himself all the time.

'Oh, Sampson Brass, if I ever see you again, I will kill you!' he cried. 'But, Sally! Why did you let him tell them? You should have stopped him! Oh, I …'

At that moment there was a knock at the door. He blew out the candle and suddenly it was quite dark. He walked through the counting-house and out through the back door to the side of the river.

'I'll climb over the wall at the end of the yard and escape,' he told himself. But as he moved in the darkness he fell. The next moment he was fighting with the cold, dark water of the river! He could still hear the knocking, and now he heard shouting. He knew the voice. Yes, it was the young boy who worked for him! Quilp moved his arms and legs wildly and tried to call out to him. But it was too late. His clothes were wet and heavy and the water pulled him down towards the bottom of the river until he stopped moving. Quilp would never move again. He was dead.

19
The Single Gentleman Shares his Story

Kit was now happier than he had ever been. He had heard the news about Mr Brass and Sally and had been told that he was now a free man. Mr Garland came as quickly as he could to get Kit from the prison and take him home.

When they arrived back at the Garlands' house Kit's mother was there with his two brothers and she was crying with joy. Mrs Garland, Abel, Barbara and the single gentleman were there too. They were all very excited and pleased to see Kit – especially Barbara. They laughed and talked and gave Kit special presents to welcome him home.

After a while, Kit realized that he had forgotten to say hello to another friend. He quietly walked out to the back of the house to the stables[67], where Whisker the pony was kept. He put his hand on Whisker's neck and spoke to him gently. As he was talking, he heard someone move behind him. It was Barbara! What was Barbara doing here?

'Oh, Kit,' she said, 'is it really you? Are you really back here safe with us? I've missed you so much.'

She was standing quite near him now and Kit could see that she had begun to cry. Without thinking about it, he put his arm around her, and dried her cheek. She looked up at him, and again without thinking, Kit kissed her. The pony suddenly moved and Barbara, who was surprised, ran away.

Later that evening, when everything was calmer, Mr Garland asked to speak to Kit.

'Would you come with me on a journey tomorrow?' he asked.

'A journey?' asked Kit.

'Yes,' replied his master. 'Nell and her grandfather have

The Single Gentleman Shares his Story

been found and we should go and see them. Nell has been ill and is weak, but I hope she will be better soon.'

Mr Garland then told Kit the whole story. He explained that he had a very good friend who was a schoolteacher who lived in a village in the country. His name was Mr Marton. He did not see this friend very often, but they wrote letters to each other. In one of his letters, Mr Marton had described helping two new people in the village – a young girl and her old grandfather. He wrote about how they had been travelling and were poor. When Mr Garland had read this he thought they might be Kit's friends, so he wrote a letter asking Mr Marton for more information. That very day a reply had come which said that yes, they were Nell and her grandfather.

Kit was very happy and said that of course he would be ready for the journey the next morning. He found it difficult to sleep that night because he was thinking about Nell, and about Barbara.

Early the next morning Mr Garland and the single gentleman climbed into the carriage. Kit climbed up onto the back of it, and they began their long journey. They travelled all day and into the evening. After a long silence in the carriage, the single gentleman turned to Mr Garland and asked him if he was a good listener.

'Yes, of course,' he replied. 'If the story is interesting!'

'Then there is a short story I want to tell you,' the single gentleman began. 'There were two brothers who loved each other a lot. There was an age difference of twelve years between them. Happily, they both fell in love, but sadly, it was with the same woman. The younger brother was the first to realize this and he was very upset about it. When he was a child he had been very ill and weak and his older brother had looked after him very carefully for years. The younger brother decided not to say anything about the woman because he wanted his brother to be happy. He left the country.

The Single Gentleman Shares his Story

'The older brother married the woman and was very happy for a while. But then his wife died and left him with a daughter. This daughter was beautiful and was exactly like her mother. She grew up to be a sweet woman, but she married a terrible man who spent all of her money and was cruel to her. They were so poor that first her husband died, and then she died too, leaving two children behind. There was a son of about ten years old and a baby girl. So then their grandfather – the older brother – looked after them. He was very sad. He had lost his wife, and then he had lost his daughter, and he was by that time an old man.

'The two children grew up to be very different. The boy became just like his father had been. He was dishonest and lazy, and he had wasted a lot of the grandfather's money before he left to live on his own. The girl was sweet and innocent, just like her beautiful mother had been. She stayed with her grandfather and helped him to run a business, which was a shop selling old curios.

'The old man loved his young granddaughter very much. Her beautiful face reminded him of his wife and his daughter. But he was very frightened that the girl would have a sad and short life like her mother and grandmother before her.

'During all these years the younger brother was travelling in many different countries all alone. No one knew why he had left England, and they thought it must have been for bad reasons. As he got older he thought more and more about his older brother and the happy times they had shared as children. The time came when he could bear it no more. He sold everything he owned. Now being rich enough to look after both himself and his brother, he returned to London and knocked on his brother's door …' said the single gentleman, whose voice had grown quiet and sad.

'Yes,' said Mr Garland, putting his hand on top of his friend's, 'And I think I know the rest of the story.'

The Single Gentleman Shares his Story

'Yes,' agreed the single gentleman. 'You know all about how I have been looking for my brother and his granddaughter and, until now, have had no luck. I really hope that this time we will find them.'

20
Nell and her Grandfather are Found

The carriage travelled on all through the next day, stopping only to change horses, or for the passengers to eat. It was a very long and tiring journey and Kit became very cold sitting at the back of the carriage. Soon it was dark again and snowing and there were many miles still to travel.

At last, at around midnight, they arrived in the small village. Kit went ahead to look for Nell's cottage and when he found it he saw a light through the window. He knocked on the door. There was no answer, but he could hear a strange noise coming from inside. It sounded like a person singing, or crying, or perhaps both. He felt cold and worried. He pushed open the door and went inside. There was a weak fire burning in the room and in front of it there was a person sitting in a chair. It was an old man who was crying and talking to himself. He looked up, and then Kit knew who it was. It was his old master from The Old Curiosity Shop!

'Master!' cried Kit, and he ran to him.

'Another ghost[68]!' said the old man.

'I'm not a ghost. I'm Kit, your old servant. Don't you remember?' asked Kit. 'Where is Nell? Oh, please tell me where Nell is.'

'There have been lots of ghosts this evening, and they have all wanted to know where she is,' the old man replied. 'She's in the next room, sleeping.'

'Oh, thank goodness!' cried Kit.

'But she has been asleep for such a long time,' said the old man weakly. 'Why do you lie there, Nell? Your friends come to the door asking, "Where is the sweet girl?" and they start crying. She is so tired that she doesn't move at all when she

Nell and her Grandfather are Found

is sleeping. She needs to rest, then she will get better. Yes, she will get better.'

Kit could not speak. He had begun to cry. A few moments passed and then the door opened and in walked Mr Garland, the single gentleman and Mr Marton. They saw how upset the old man was and heard from Kit what he had said about his granddaughter.

The single gentleman – the old man's younger brother – walked slowly to him and began to speak.

'I know that you are tired and very upset about little Nell. And I know that you must still be sad about the death of her mother and grandmother. You loved them all. But do you remember another person who you once loved – your brother? You used to look after him and you shared a happy childhood together. But then he left home to travel the world. Imagine if that brother returned now, to look after you, just as you had looked after him before.' He stopped for a moment before saying gently, 'Do you recognize me, good brother?'

The old grandfather looked at all the people in the room and began to move slowly towards the room where Nell lay. As he moved he spoke.

'You are trying to make me forget her. You will never do that. She is the only friend or relative I have. She is everything to me,' he said as he walked into her room, gently calling her name.

The others, who were worried about him, followed him quietly into Nell's room. They all felt very sad and more than one of them was crying.

Nell was dead. She lay on the little bed, white and not moving.

The old man did not want to believe it. He held her hand, the same hand that had led him on their long journey, and said that he needed to keep it warm. But it was too late. Sweet, kind Nell was dead.

Kit could not speak. He had begun to cry.

Nell and her Grandfather are Found

She had been dead for two days. When she died there had been friends around her, and she had died quietly and without any pain. She had never complained and had been thankful to everyone who looked after her. They said that she had often spoken of the people who had been kind to her. She had said more than once that she would like to see Kit again. She wished that someone would tell Kit that she loved and missed him.

———

The day of the funeral[69] came and many people from the village, all of them dressed in black, came to say goodbye to Nell. She was buried in the same churchyard that she had looked after herself. Just as she had planted flowers on the graves of children there, her friends did the same for her grave.

After the funeral, Nell's grandfather was taken back to the cottage. He went into Nell's room to look for her, but of course she was gone and he was very upset. He then went to Mr Marton the schoolteacher's house to look for her there. He could not, *would* not, believe that she had died.

The days passed and he spent every day sitting by her grave, waiting for her return. His friends and his brother tried everything they could to make him understand that she had gone. Sadly, several weeks later, on a sunny spring day, they found him lying dead on her grave. He was buried next to her, and so, at last, Nell and her grandfather were together again, just as he had wanted.

21
The End

The story of Nell and her poor grandfather has now come to its end. All that is left to do is to tell you what happened to the other people who have been part of this sad story.

Mr Brass's trial was held, but because he was a lawyer and knew all the right people, he was not transported to a country far away. He was sent to quite a nice prison for a few years and he never worked as a lawyer again.

No one was sure what happened to Sally Brass. Some people said she had dressed as a man and gone to sea as a sailor. Others said that she had become a soldier. But the truth was that she had just disappeared, and nobody knew where she was.

Daniel Quilp's body was found several days after he had fallen into the river. There was an inquest[70], but there was no funeral and no one cared that he was dead.

Mr and Mrs Garland carried on their lives as before, but with fewer people in their house, as you will see. Their son, Abel, went to a dance where he met a very quiet lady and fell in love. In a few months he was happily married and in a few years he had a quiet family too.

Richard Swiveller slowly recovered from his illness and received the money that his rich aunt had left to him. He was a changed man. As he had promised, he used the money to look after the Marchioness. He bought her some wonderful new clothes and paid for her to go to school. She was very clever and became an excellent student.

The younger brother, or single gentleman as we knew him, was full of sadness at what had happened. He set out on a long journey – the same journey that Nell and his older brother had

The End

followed after they had left London. He took the time to find and thank every person who had helped them on their way.

And what about Kit? Kit's story had been heard by a lot of people. At first he had no plan to leave Mr and Mrs Garland, but a stranger offered him an excellent job and everyone agreed that he should take it. Did Kit live as a single man for all his days, or did he get married? Of course he got married, and of course it was Barbara that became his wife! They were happy together and had two children.

As Kit's children grew up he would often tell them the story of little Nell. He told them how good and sweet and kind she had been. He sometimes took them to the street where she had lived. But it had changed a lot and looked very different. A new, wide road was in its place. The Old Curiosity Shop was no longer there. It had been pulled down a long time ago. At first he would show them the exact spot where the shop had stood. But soon he became unsure and could not find the place where it had been. So much had changed and his memory was not what it had been.

These are the changes that can happen over a few years. Things pass away and are forgotten, just like a story that has been told!

Points For Understanding

1

1 Two people lived at The Old Curiosity Shop. What was their relationship to each other?
2 'The old man's face was full of worry and sadness.' What was the old man worried and sad about?
3 Who had Kit just visited and why?
4 Nell started to cry near the end of this chapter. Why?

2

1 Two unwanted visitors arrived at The Old Curiosity Shop.
  (a) Who were they? (b) Why had they come?
2 Why had Daniel Quilp come to The Old Curiosity Shop?
3 Nell's grandfather said twice that he hoped something would happen. What did he want to happen?
4 There was another visitor who was very welcome.
  (a) Who was that person? (b) Why had that person come?

3

1 Fred Trent made a surprising suggestion in this chapter.
  (a) What was the suggestion?
  (b) What reasons did Fred give to support his idea?
2 What was Richard Swiveller's first reaction to Fred's suggestion?
3 By the end of the chapter, Richard changed his mind about Fred's plan. What made him change his mind?
4 What do you think of Richard Swiveller?

4

1 'It's all gone already? In just twenty-four hours! What on earth has he done with it?' What was the 'it' that Quilp was referring to?
2 Nell reported what her grandfather had said to her: 'I can't believe how unlucky I've been with the cards I've been dealt.' (a) What do you think Nell thought he meant when he said that? (b) What do you think her grandfather really meant by it?
3 This chapter is called 'Quilp Uncovers a Secret'. What was the secret that was uncovered?
4 Quilp told a lie near the end of this chapter. (a) What was the lie? (b) Why do you think Quilp told this lie?

5

1 Kit experienced many different emotions in this chapter. Describe two of the feelings he had and why he felt them.
2 Why did Nell start to cry (page 23)?
3 What suggestion did Nell make to her grandfather? Did he agree to the suggestion?
4 'She thought of the sun and rivers and green grass and summer days, and there were no dark corners in the picture she saw.' What do you think this means?

6

1 Nell and her grandfather met two men in this chapter. (a) What were their names? (b) Why were they sitting in a churchyard?
2 Nell hid something in this chapter. (a) What did she hide? (b) Where did she hide it? (c) Why did she hide it?

3 'She no longer felt safe after what she had heard them say.' (a) What had Nell heard? (b) What did she decide to do?

7

1 In this chapter three people had different reactions to the disappearance of Nell and her grandfather. (a) Who was 'not very surprised' and why? (b) Who was 'shocked and upset' and why? (c) Who was 'truly sad' and why?
2 Quilp told another lie in this chapter. What lie did he tell and why did he tell it?
3 The little old gentleman with the pony and carriage laughed when he gave Kit a sixpence. Explain why the man laughed, and why Kit was serious.

8

1 Nell and her grandfather met a man who helped them in this chapter. (a) What was his name? (b) What was his job? (c) How did he help them?
2 Later in the chapter Nell and her grandfather met a woman who helped them. (a) What did she look like? (b) How did she travel? (c) How did she help them?

9

1 'They sat in silence for a few minutes while Mrs Jarley spent some time thinking.' What do you think Mrs Jarley was thinking?
2 At first, Nell did not accept the job she was offered. Why not?
3 What did Nell have to do in her job?

10

1 'She looked at her grandfather and was worried to see he had changed.' What changes did Nell see in her grandfather and what had caused them?
2 'I didn't mean to upset you. I only want to do this for you, to look after you!' What was it that Nell's grandfather wanted to do?
3 'Nell had been frightened, but now she felt sick.' Why had Nell been frightened and what made her feel sick?

11

1 Dickens wanted to make the description of Sally Brass funny. Why does the phrase 'all these attractive qualities' make the reader laugh?
2 This chapter is called 'Richard Gets a Job'. What job did Richard get and who helped him to get the job? Why do you think he helped Richard?
3 How much money did the single gentleman give Richard and what was it for?

12

1 What question did the single gentleman ask Tommy Codlin and Mr Harris? What was their reply?
2 'Why on earth would these two be together?'
(a) Who asked himself this question? (b) Who were 'these two'? (c) What was the answer to this question?
3 The single gentleman wanted Kit to go on a journey with him. (a) Where did he want to go? (b) Why did Kit refuse to go too? (c) What did Kit suggest instead?

13

1. What did the gamblers want Nell's grandfather to do?
2. Why do you think Nell did not like the town they arrived in?
3. Why did Nell suddenly scream and fall to the ground in shock?
4. What suggestion did Mr Marton make near the end of this chapter?

14

1. How had Mrs Jarley felt when Nell and her grandfather disappeared?
2. Who was the single gentleman angry with in this chapter and why?
3. Quilp said, 'I think I will have to kill him.'
   (a) Who was Quilp talking about? (b) Why did he want to get rid of him? (c) How did he plan to do it?

15

1. 'Thank you so much!' said Nell. Who did she thank and why?
2. What was Nell given in this chapter and why?
3. Both Mr Marton and Nell's grandfather became worried when they saw that she was only working on the graves of children. (a) Why do you think they were worried?
   (b) What evidence is there to show what her grandfather might have been thinking?

16

1 'Kit, that was a painful job for me!' said Mr Brass to Kit. What 'job' was he referring to and why do you think he wanted to tell Kit how he felt about it then?
2 In this chapter Richard Swiveller became friends with the servant-girl. What facts tell the reader that the servant-girl had not been well looked after?
3 Six things had 'disappeared' or 'gone missing' in this chapter. What were these items?
4 Mr Brass called Kit into his office twice in this chapter. Where were the following people both times this happened? (a) Richard Swiveller (b) Sally (c) the single gentleman
5 Mr Brass and Sally told a lot of lies in this chapter. Summarize what their plan was and how they put the plan into action.

17

1 Quilp wanted to 'get rid of' Richard Swiveller in this chapter. Why?
2 Kit's mother was 'very upset and could not stop crying'. Why?
3 What caused Richard to be 'shocked and angry'?
4 What caused the Marchioness to 'cry with joy'?
5 'Kit really was innocent!' What new information was there in this chapter that would help to prove this?

18

1. Why was Sally Brass invited to the coffee-house?
2. Two letters were mentioned in this chapter. (a) Who were they written by? (b) Who were they sent to? (c) What information did each letter contain?
3. The title of the chapter is 'Quilp's Luck Changes'. What happened to Quilp at the end of the chapter?

19

1. Explain the relationship between Mr Garland and Mr Marton. Why was this relationship important for the story?
2. Who was the single gentleman and why did he want to find Nell and her grandfather?
3. The single gentleman also told us more about Nell's grandfather. What did we learn about him that we did not know before?

20

1. Nell's grandfather said that Nell's friends had come to the cottage and cried. Why do you think they cried?
2. The single gentleman explained to Nell's grandfather who he was and why he was there. How did Nell's grandfather respond to this news?
3. 'The others, who were worried about him, followed him quietly into Nell's room.' Name the people who were present when they went into Nell's room.
4. After the funeral, Nell's grandfather went to Nell's bedroom and then to Mr Marton's house. Why?

21

1 'Mr and Mrs Garland carried on their lives as before, but with fewer people in their house.' Who left their house and why?
2 What did Richard Swiveller do with the money that he inherited?
3 Where did Kit often take his children and why?
4 The story ends with the sentence, 'Things pass away and are forgotten, just like a story that has been told!' What 'things' do you think the author meant?

Glossary

1. **clerk** (page 4)
   someone whose job is to look after the documents in an office, court, etc.
2. **begging** – *to beg someone to do something* (page 5)
   If you *beg* someone to do something, you ask them in a way that shows you want it very much. If you ask people for money or food, usually because you are very poor, you *beg*. Someone who is very poor and lives by asking people for money or food is called a *beggar*.
3. **docks** (page 5)
   an enclosed area of water in a port, where ships stay while goods are taken on or off, passengers get on or off or repairs are done. Ports usually have *wharfs* (structures for boats to stop at, at the edge of the land or leading from the land out into the water) and *boatyards* (places for making, repairing or keeping boats).
4. **bear** – *cannot bear to do something* (page 5)
   if you cannot *bear* to do something, you cannot do it because it makes you very unhappy
5. **servant** (page 6)
   someone whose job is to cook, clean or do other work in someone else's home
6. **carriage** (page 6)
   a vehicle with wheels that is pulled by horses, especially one used in the past before cars were invented. Carriages were pulled by one, two or four horses and were sometimes called *coaches*.
7. **waxworks** (page 7)
   a place where people can see a collection of models of famous people made from *wax* – a soft, natural or artificial substance that becomes liquid when heated

8 *gentleman* (page 7)
   an old word for a man from a family in a high social class. A woman from a high social class was called a *lady*.
9 *Marchioness* (page 7)
   the title given to a British noblewoman of the second-highest social class, just below a duchess, or the title of a woman married to a marquess. The name is a joke because the servant-girl is small and thin and very poor.
10 *waste* – *to waste something* (page 8)
   to fail to make effective use of something that is valuable
11 *candle* (page 9)
   a stick of wax with a string in it called a wick that you burn to give light. If you *light* a candle, you make it burn, and the place where a candle is burning is described as *candlelit*.
12 *master* (page 9)
   a man who has control over servants or other people who work for him
13 *cloak* (page 9)
   a long, thick, loose coat without sleeves, that fastens around your neck
14 *tear* (page 9)
   a drop of liquid that comes from your eye when you cry. In this story, the people cry *tears of sadness* when they are sad and *tears of joy* when they are happy.
15 *handsome* (page 11)
   a *handsome* man or boy has a very attractive face
16 *arrogant* (page 11)
   someone who is *arrogant* thinks they are better or more important than other people and behaves in a way that is rude and too confident

17 *shilling* (page 11)
   an old-fashioned coin. A *coin* is a flat, round piece of metal with special designs on it, used as money. There are a lot of different old coins in the story. These were the units of money used in the past in the UK. A *sixpence* was a coin that was the same as six old pennies. A *shilling* was the same as twelve old pennies. A *half crown* was the same as two-and-a-half shillings. There were twelve shillings, or eight half crowns, in a pound. A piece of money made from paper is called a *banknote* or a *note*.
18 *criticize* – *to criticize someone or something* (page 11)
   to say what you think is wrong or bad about someone or something
19 *liar* (page 11)
   someone who tells lies
20 *winked* – *to wink at someone* (page 12)
   to quickly close and open one eye as a sign to someone, for example a sign that what you have just said is a joke or a secret
21 *simple* (page 12)
   a *simple* life is a life that is honest and ordinary
22 *rough* (page 12)
   with a surface that is not smooth or soft to touch
23 *roughly* (page 13)
   in a way that is not gentle
24 *disgusted* (page 13)
   feeling strongly that you do not like something
25 *selfish* (page 13)
   thinking only about yourself and not caring about other people

26 *investment* (page 15)
If you use your money with the aim of making a profit from it, you *invest* it. For example, you buy property or buy shares in a company. Something that you are willing to spend money on now because it will give you benefits in the future is called an *investment*.

27 *stared* – *to stare at someone* (page 17)
to look at someone or something very directly for a long time

28 *ignore* – *to ignore someone or something* (page 17)
to pretend that you have not noticed someone or something

29 *bat* (page 17)
a small animal that flies at night and looks like a mouse with large wings. A bat cannot see very well.

30 *persuaded* – *to persuade someone to do something* (page 18)
to make someone agree to do something by giving them reasons why they should. Someone who is good at persuading people to do things is *persuasive*.

31 *inherit* – *to inherit something* (page 18)
to receive property or money from someone who has died. The money or property that you receive is called an *inheritance*.

32 *greedy* (page 18)
wanting more money, things or power than you need

33 *illegal* (page 19)
not allowed by the law

34 *managed* – *to manage to do something* (page 19)
to succeed in doing something, especially something that needs a lot of effort or skill

35 *gambling* – *to gamble* (page 21)
to risk money or something valuable in the hope of winning more if you are lucky, for example in a game of cards. Someone who gambles is called a *gambler*.

36 *security* (page 22)
property or goods that you agree to give to someone who has lent you money if you cannot pay the money back
37 *shadow* (page 23)
an area of darkness that is created when something blocks light
38 *widowed* (page 23)
if someone is *widowed*, their husband or wife has died
39 *shocked* (page 24)
very surprised and upset by something bad that happens unexpectedly
40 *despite* (page 24)
a word used to join parts of a sentence for saying that something happens (one part of the sentence) even though something else might have prevented it (the other part)
41 *pleasant* (page 24)
a *pleasant* person is friendly and behaves correctly in social situations. A *pleasant* place is enjoyable or attractive in a way that makes you feel happy.
42 *confused* (page 25)
used for describing someone whose memory or mental powers are starting to fail
43 *led* – *to lead someone or something* (page 26)
to take or pull a person or animal somewhere by holding onto them or onto something fastened to them
44 *rough* (page 27)
houses that look *rough* are dirty and in a bad condition

45 *puppet* (page 27)
   a small model of a person or animal that you can move by pulling wires or strings, or by putting your hand inside it. Someone who performs shows using puppets is called a *puppeteer*. Puppet shows were very popular in England at the time when Dickens wrote the story, and puppeteers travelled around the country to give shows in the streets of towns and villages.

46 *public house* (page 29)
   a place where people go to drink alcohol, especially in the UK and Ireland. These days, it is usually called a *pub*. A *public house* is run by a *landlord* or *landlady*.

47 *sewed* – *to sew* (page 29)
   to use a small, thin metal tool called a needle and a long, thin fibre called a thread to make or repair clothes or to join two pieces of cloth together

48 *reward* (page 30)
   money that someone receives for finding and returning something or for helping the police

49 *stubborn* (page 32)
   a *stubborn* animal refuses to do what you want it to do

50 *pony* (page 32)
   a small horse

51 *ma'am* (page 38)
   used in the past for talking politely to a woman whose name you do not know. It comes from the word *madam*.

52 *grabbed* – *to grab something* (page 42)
   to take hold of something in a rough or rude way

53 *client* (page 45)
   someone who pays for the services of a professional person such as a doctor or lawyer

54 *cellar* (page 46)
   a room under a building, below the level of the ground, usually used for storing things

55 *lodger* (page 47)
someone who pays to live in part of someone else's house. The rooms that the lodger lives in are called his or her *lodgings*.

56 *enquiry* (page 49)
a question intended to get information about someone or something

57 *get rid of* – *to get rid of someone* (page 56)
to make someone go away because they are annoying, unpleasant or not wanted

58 *clergyman* (page 57)
a man who leads religious services, especially a Christian priest

59 *grave* (page 57)
the place where a dead body is buried in a deep hole in the ground. The place next to a church where there are graves is called the *churchyard* or the *graveyard*.

60 *painful* (page 59)
making you feel upset, ashamed or unhappy

61 *statement* (page 63)
a formal written account of events that a person who has seen a crime or who has been accused of a crime gives to the police

62 *magistrate* (page 63)
a judge in a court for minor crimes

63 *justice-room* (page 65)
the place where the legal process of deciding whether someone is *guilty* – that they have committed a crime – takes place. If someone is *found guilty*, they are *sentenced* – the judge states what their *punishment* will be. A punishment is a way in which someone is made to suffer because they have done something wrong, for example by going to prison or, in the past, by being *transported* – sent by boat to live in a different place or country.

64 *trial* (page 66)
the process of examining a case in a court of law and deciding whether someone is guilty

65 *proof* (page 68)
information or evidence that shows that something is definitely true or definitely exists

66 *arrest* (page 69)
if the police *arrest* someone, they take that person to a police station because they believe he or she has committed a crime. The action of arresting someone is an *arrest*. A *warrant for someone's arrest* is a document written by a judge that gives the police permission to arrest someone.

67 *stable* (page 71)
a building where horses or farm animals are kept

68 *ghost* (page 75)
the spirit of a dead person that someone believes they see or hear

69 *funeral* (page 78)
a ceremony that takes place after someone dies, often including a religious ceremony, and the formal process of taking the body to the place where it is buried or burnt

70 *inquest* (page 79)
an official attempt by a court to find the cause of someone's death

Useful Phrases

I am breaking my heart over – *to break one's heart over something* (page 5)
to be very upset about something

once and for all (page 13)
completely and finally

he kept his eyes open – *to keep one's eyes open for something* (page 19)
to keep looking for someone or something that you hope to find

What on earth …? (page 20)
we use *on earth* with *What/Why/How/Where …?* questions to add emphasis

I can't believe how unlucky I've been with the cards I've been dealt (page 20)
in a game of cards, the *cards you are dealt* are the cards you are given to play with. This expression is also used in general to talk about the situation you are in in your life. Someone who is unlucky with the cards they have been dealt has a lot of problems and difficulties. We do not know if Nell's grandfather is talking about card games or real life.

to make your fortune (page 21)
if you make your fortune, you become very rich

keeping an eye on – *to keep an eye on someone or something* (page 23)
to look after someone or something

play a trick on – *to play a trick on someone* (page 31)
to make someone believe something that is not true

try his luck – *to try your luck* (page 47)
to try something that may not be successful

in advance (page 47)
if you pay for something *in advance*, you give the money before you receive the goods or service

getting in my way – *to get in someone's way* (page 55)
to stop someone from doing something, either without realizing you are doing it or because you want to stop them

Let's shake hands on it – *to shake hands on something* (page 56)
if you shake hands with someone on something, you show that you both agree to something. Sometimes it is used to mean you agree but you do not actually shake hands.

Glossary and Useful Phrases definitions from the Macmillan English Dictionary 2nd Edition
© *Macmillan Publishers Limited 2007* www.macmillandictionary.com

Exercises

Background Information

Read 'A Note About The Author' and 'A Note About The Story'. Write T (True) or F (False).

1 Charles Dickens was born in Portsmouth, England.   *T*
2 His father was a very rich man.
3 Charles Dickens went to prison when he was twelve.
4 After his father went to prison, Dickens left school.
5 He started writing stories when he was fifteen.
6 *The Old Curiosity Shop* was not his first novel.
7 Dickens was buried in London.
8 When this novel was first published it was not popular.
9 Dickens often wrote about poor children.
10 The story is set at the end of the nineteenth century.

People in the Story

Write a name from the box next to the correct information below.

> Daniel Quilp   Fred Trent   Kit   Mr and Mrs Garland
> Mr Brass   Mr Marton   Mrs Jarley   ~~Nell~~
> Nell's grandfather   Richard Swiveller
> The Marchioness   Tommy Codlin

1   *Nell* is a thirteen-year-old girl.
2   .... owns The Old Curiosity Shop.
3   .... is Nell's older brother.
4   .... is Nell's friend and works in the shop.
5   .... lends money and owns a boatyard.
6   .... is a friend of Nell's brother.
7   .... is Daniel Quilp's lawyer.
8   .... is a schoolteacher who helps Nell.
9   .... are an old couple who Kit goes to work for.
10 .... is the owner of a travelling waxworks.
11 .... is a servant-girl who works for Mr Brass and Sally.
12 .... is a travelling entertainer.

Multiple Choice

Tick the best answer.

1 When Nell's grandfather went out late at night …
   a Kit stayed in the shop with Nell.
   b he locked the door after he left.
   c Nell stayed in the shop alone. ✓
   d he told Nell where he was going.

2 Who did Nell's grandfather borrow gold from?
   a Daniel Quilp
   b Fred Trent
   c Kit
   d Richard Swiveller

3 What did Nell's grandfather do with the gold?
   a He hid it.
   b He gambled with it.
   c He gave it to Nell.
   d He invested it.

4 What did Nell and her grandfather do after he got better?
   a They went to stay with Kit's family.
   b They borrowed money from Daniel Quilp.
   c They left The Old Curiosity Shop.
   d They asked Kit to work for them again.

5 Mr Garland offered Kit a job because …
   a he needed a servant.
   b he thought Kit was poor.
   c Kit was Nell's friend.
   d he thought Kit was honest.

6 The job Mrs Jarley gave to Nell was to …
   a tell the crowds about the waxworks.
   b look after the caravan.
   c keep the waxworks clean.
   d find Daniel Quilp.

7 Nell was very sad after the night at the public house because …
   a they did not have any money.
   b her grandfather lost money playing cards.
   c he stole some money from her room.
   d he was happy when he was gambling.

8 What did the single gentleman ask Kit to do?
   a help him find Nell and her grandfather
   b keep an eye on Daniel Quilp
   c talk to Richard Swiveller
   d rent a room to him in his house

9 What did Quilp decide to do after he met the single gentleman in the public house?
   a find Nell and her grandfather
   b talk to Fred Trent
   c find Kit and hurt him
   d find Kit and offer him a job

10 Who lied about the money that went missing?
   a Kit
   b Mr Brass and Sally
   c Richard Swiveller
   d Mr Garland

11 What happened to Quilp after he read the letter from Sally Brass?
   a He was arrested.
   b He tried to find Sally and her brother.
   c He fell into the river and drowned.
   d He ran away.

12 Who was the single gentleman?
   a Nell's father
   b the brother of Nell's grandfather
   c Nell's brother
   d Mr Garland's younger brother

13 What was wrong when Kit found Nell's grandfather?
   a He was already dead.
   b Nell was dead.
   c Nell was sleeping because she was very ill.
   d He was upset because Nell had run away.

14 At the end of the story who is sent to prison?
   a Daniel Quilp
   b Richard Swiveller
   c Sally Brass
   d Sampson Brass

Vocabulary: Anagrams

Write the letters in the correct order to make words from the story.

1	ETNALMENG	*gentleman*	an old word for a man from a family of high class
2	VARENTS		someone whose job is to cook, clean or do other work in someone else's home
3	TREAMS		a man who has control over servants or other people who work for him
4	OGDREL		someone who pays to live in part of someone else's house
5	RELCK		someone whose job is to look after documents in an office, court, etc.
6	LICTEN		someone who pays for the services of a professional person such as a doctor or lawyer
7	GLARMCENY		a man who leads religious services, especially a Christian priest
8	ITREGAMATS		a judge in a court for minor crimes

Words from the Story

Complete the gaps. Use each word in the box once.

arrogant ~~confused~~ disgusted greedy
ignore inherit persuaded proof reward selfish
shadows stubborn

1 After his illness Nell's grandfather was *confused* and often said things that did not make sense.

2 Fred Trent was very .... because he behaved as though he was better than everyone else.

3 Fred was a .... young man who always thought about himself and not other people.

4 'Do you think there's a ....?' he asked. 'We will get some money if we bring her back.'

5 'All you think about is having lots of money,' he said. 'You're so ....!'

6 When Nell saw Quilp she hid in the .... and watched him secretly.

7 'I don't believe he stole the money. Do you have any .... that it was him?'

8 'Why did you .... me?' asked Richard angrily. 'You knew I was there.'

9 She never wants to do what we say. She's so ....

10 Richard Swiveller hoped he would .... some money when his aunt died.

11 At first, Richard did not like the plan to marry Nell but Fred .... him that it was a good idea.

12 Quilp was .... by the way Fred Trent treated his grandfather.

Useful Phrases

Match the verbs on the left with the words on the right to make phrases from the story.

1 keep	a a trick on someone
2 break	b hands on something
3 make	c one's eyes open for something
4 keep	d one's heart over something
5 play	e in someone's way
6 try	f your fortune
7 get	g an eye on someone
8 shake	h your luck

1 → c

Choose the correct phrases from the table above to match the definitions.

9 not stop looking for something you want to find
keep one's eyes open for something

10 agree to something

11 attempt something that might not be successful

12 be very upset about something

13 become very rich

14 look after someone

15 make someone believe something that is not true

16 stop someone from doing something

Grammar: Reporting verbs

Circle the correct reporting verb.

1 'You know that I love you, Nell,' said / told the old man.
2 'Of course I do,' Nell asked / replied.
3 'Did you give the letter to Daniel Quilp.' asked / replied the old man.
4 'I'm sure there's a reward,' asked / whispered Mr Harris to Tommy Codlin.
5 'I have a very good friend,' explained / told Mr Garland, 'who sent me a letter.'
6 'Now you must get rid of him,' he asked / told Mr Brass.
7 'I've been abroad for many years,' the single gentleman said / told Kit.
8 'Master!' cried / explained Kit.
9 'Don't you remember me?' he asked / told.
10 'She's very weak and ill,' he said / told her grandfather.

Grammar: Relative pronouns

Circle the correct word to complete the sentences.

1 The old man, ... was alone in the shop, was not pleased to see Fred.

   a where **b** which **c** (who) **d** whose

2 They walked into the town, ... was noisy and full of factories.

   a where **b** which **c** who **d** whose

3 He saw an old man with long, grey hair, ... face looked tired and sad.

   a where **b** which **c** who **d** whose

4 Nell was taken upstairs to bed, ... she slept for several hours.

   a where **b** which **c** who **d** whose

5 Richard Swiveller, ... could not believe what he had just heard, spoke one word.

   a where **b** which **c** who **d** whose

6 Kit walked quickly to the stables, ... Whisker the pony was kept.

   a where **b** which **c** who **d** whose

7 Kit, ... face was starting to turn red, was saved by a loud knock at the door.

   a where **b** which **c** who **d** whose

8 It was a smart little house on wheels, ... was painted brightly.

   a where **b** which **c** who **d** whose

Grammar: Adverbs

Complete the gaps. Use each adverb in the box once.

> immediately   just   never   often   only   recently
> still   ~~suddenly~~   unusually

1 Then _suddenly_ she woke up. It was dark, but she could see someone standing in her room.

2 She recognized him .... It was the ugly, frightening Quilp.

3 They were .... beginning to get worried when they saw a caravan at the side of the road.

4 It was now very late and the storm was .... blowing outside.

5 They noticed that Nell .... worked on the children's graves.

6 In this story we .... find out the name of Nell's grandfather.

7 When Kit's children were growing up he would .... tell them the story about little Nell.

8 'You've brought a lot of letters to me ...., haven't you, Nell?' Quilp said coldly.

9 Kit was a shy boy with red cheeks, an .... wide mouth and a turned-up nose.

Pronunciation: Word stress

Write the two-syllable and three-syllable words in the box in the correct column according to the main stress.

arrogant   confused   criticize   disgusted   ignore   inherit   innocent   inquest   investment   persuaded   ~~pleasant~~   pretend   reward   selfish   shadow   terribly

●●	●●	●●●	●●●
pleasant			

Visit the Macmillan Readers website at
www.macmillanenglish.com/readers

*to find **FREE resources** for use in class and for independent learning. Search our **online catalogue** to buy new Readers including **audio download** and **eBook** versions.*

Here's a taste of what's available:

For the classroom:

- **Tests** for most Readers to check understanding and monitor progress
- **Worksheets** for most Readers to explore language and themes
- **Listening worksheets** to practise extensive listening
- Worksheets to help prepare for the **First** (**FCE) reading exam**

Additional resources for students and independent learners:

- An **online level test** to identify reading level
- **Author information sheets** to provide in-depth biographical information about our Readers authors
- **Self-study worksheets** to help track and record your reading which can be used with any Reader
- Use our **creative writing worksheets** to help you write short stories, poetry and biographies
- Write academic essays and literary criticism confidently with the help of our **academic writing worksheets**
- Have fun completing our **webquests** and **projects** and learn more about the Reader you are studying
- Go backstage and read **interviews** with **famous authors** and **actors**
- Discuss your favourite Readers at the **Book Corner Club**

Visit *www.macmillanenglish.com/readers* **to find out more!**

Macmillan Education Limited
4 Crinan Street
London N1 9XW

Companies and representatives throughout the world

ISBN 978-0-230-46038-6
ISBN 978-0-230-46041-6 (with CD edition)

Text, design and illustration © Macmillan Education Limited 2014
This version of *The Old Curiosity Shop* by Charles Dickens was retold by
Helen Holwill for Macmillan Readers.

The original author and the adapter have asserted their rights to be
identified as the authors of this work in accordance with the Copyright,
Designs and Patents Act 1988.

First published 2014

All rights reserved; no part of this publication may be reproduced, stored
in a retrieval system, transmitted in any form, or by any means, electronic,
mechanical, photocopying, recording, or otherwise, without the prior
written permission of the publishers.

Designed by Carolyn Gibson
Illustrated by Jérôme Brasseur
Cover photograph by Getty Images / Science & Society Picture Library

These materials may contain links for third party websites. We have no
control over, and are not responsible for, the contents of such third party
websites. Please use care when accessing them.

Although we have tried to trace and contact copyright holders before
publication, in some cases this has not been possible. If contacted we will
be pleased to rectify any errors or omissions at the earliest opportunity.

Printed and bound in the UK by CLOC Ltd
without CD edition
2023   2022
9   8

with CD edition
2019   2018   2017   2016   2015   2014
10   9   8   7   6   5   4   3   2   1